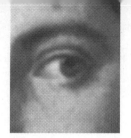

AQUINAS

③
- Aristotle's
teachings were
secular but
there was much
that fit w/the
Christian faith.
Thomas wanted to
show how they
(theology and
philosophy)
could be
combined.
Aristotle wanted to know
why things happened instead
of just how (p. 33)

- 2 biggest influences
in his life were
① the Dominican order
of ~~monks~~ Friars.
They were seen as
                    called
the dogs of the Lord.
And his family tried
to keep him away from
them.

For Leo Elders

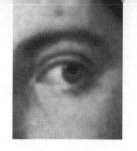

AQUINAS

— Ralph McInerny —

polity

First published in 2004 by Polity Press in association with Blackwell Publishing Ltd.

Editorial office:
Polity Press
65 Bridge Street
Cambridge CB2 1UR, UK

Marketing and production:
Blackwell Publishing Ltd
108 Cowley Road
Oxford OX4 1JF, UK

Distributed in the USA by
Blackwell Publishing Inc.
350 Main Street
Malden, MA 02148-, USA

A catalogue record for this book is available from the British Library.

Library of Congress Cataloging-in-Publication Data

McInerny, Ralph M.
Aquinas / Ralph McInerny.
    p.   cm.
Includes bibliographical references and index. ISBN 0-7456-2686-6 (alk. paper) – ISBN 0-7456-2687-4 (pbk. : alk. paper)
1. Thomas, Aquinas, Saint, 1225?–1274.   I. Title.
B765.T54 M235 2003
189′.4–dc21
        2003007462

Typeset in 10.5 on 12.5 pt Berling by SNP Best-set Typesetter Ltd.,
Hong Kong
Printed and bound in Great Britain by MPG Books, Bodmin, Cornwall

For further information on Polity, visit our website: *www.polity.co.uk*

Contents

CONTENTS

CONTENTS

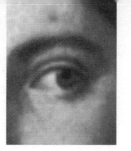

— Part I —

A Short Life

1

Origins

Thomas Aquinas was born in 1225, in the family castle at Roccasecca. Forty-nine years later on March 7, 1274, he died at Fossanova, perhaps 20 kilometers distant from his birthplace. Between those two events he had lived in Naples, Cologne, Paris, Rome, Orvieto, Viterbo, Paris again, and finally Naples. When he died, Thomas was on his way to a council that had been called in Lyon. He fell ill, was nursed by a niece in the neighborhood of whose castle he had been stricken, and then was moved to the Cistercian monastery at Fossanova where he died.

That is the first thing to know about Thomas. This scholar, this contemplative, seemed to be ever on the move. And travel was not easy. It is thought that when he went to France Thomas took a boat from Livorno and sailed to the Riviera, and then made his way up the Rhône Valley. If so, this would have spared him the hazard of Alpine passage. There is even a story that Thomas visited London, but we have no evidence of this. Not that we need another voyage to establish Thomas as a much-traveled man. If one were to trace on a map his various journeys – as those of St Paul are traced – the point would be made dramatically. In an age of planes, trains, and automobiles we must think away these alleged conveniences and imagine walking from Paris to Rome, say. In *The Path to Rome*, Hilaire Belloc writes of his own walking journey but the walk seems to have been the point, not just a means of getting somewhere. But Thomas was always hurrying to a new destination for a purpose. More likely than not on foot, perhaps on mule – he is said to have been riding a mule at the time of the accident that led to his eventual death – for portions of a journey, and, as has been mentioned, by boat.

There still is a town called Roccasecca, on the west side of the autostrada along which the latter-day countrymen of Thomas hurtle between Naples and Rome, a journey of hours now rather than days. (In Thomas's time this would still have been the *Via Latina*, the coastal road being the *Via Appia*.) On the east side of the autostrada, visible to traffic for miles, is the commanding white pile of Monte-cassino, the great Benedictine Abbey, where Thomas received his early schooling. Actually, the present-day monastery is a facsimile of the one Thomas knew, something of a Disneyland version. Its pre-decessor was bombarded during World War II when Germans dug in around the monastery and prevented the movement of the Allies to Rome. In one of the tragic moments of a tragic century, the order was given to fire upon the monastery. Photographs of the result are hung in the rebuilt monastery. The whole thing raises a moral problem of a kind Thomas would have been eager to discuss.

If you went in the other direction from the autostrada, toward Roccasecca, you would come upon a modern town, the entrance to which is flanked by advertisements of car dealers, appliances, and the like. Nothing looks very old. It isn't. If you look to the north you will see a hill town, also called Roccasecca. It has been around a good while and you may think that you have found Thomas's home town. Not quite. The family castle is further up that hill from the older town; we are only halfway to it. It is a steep and rocky climb. Goats feed on it, guarded by dogs and a goatherd. At the very top are the ruins of the castle in which Thomas Aquinas was born and in which he lived the first five years of his life. Half walls, broken archways, bushes, and bramble. But the view! You can look out over the valley, and on a clear day perhaps Montecassino would be visible in the dis-tance. Nothing brings home our littleness like the immensity of mountains. One of the stories told about Thomas is that as a young child he asked what God is. You can imagine the question forming as he looked out at the magnificent scenery.

Not that life was peaceful. Until the middle of the nineteenth century the pope was a secular prince as well as head of the church. The papal states were concentrated more or less in the middle of the peninsula. South, where Thomas was born, the Hohenstaufen emperor Frederick II held sway and he and the pope were often at war. Thomas's family were on the side of the emperor. We find all this confusing. It was pretty confusing at the time. We will come back to the significance of this for Thomas's life.

2

Montecassino (1230–1239)

When Thomas was sent to Montecassino at the age of five, he began his education in a system that had characterized medieval teaching since the Dark Ages. With the collapse of the Roman Empire and the education system it had extended across Europe, what are called the Dark Ages began. St Augustine had taught in imperial rhetorical schools, in his native Africa, in Rome, then in Milan, and as he prepared for baptism at Cassiciacum, having been swayed by the preaching of St Ambrose, he composed dialogs that give us a sense of what and how he taught. His *On Music* covers literature as well as music. His *On the Teacher* provides a sense of the presuppositions of the relationship between master and pupil. But it was a century later, when libraries were to be found for the most part in monasteries, fragments shored against the ruin of Greek culture, that the charter for monastic schools was written by Cassiodorus Senator. The *Institutions* were written for the monks at Vivarium, a monastery founded by the layman Cassiodorus, and in it he sets out the relationship between secular and sacred learning. Secular learning consists of the seven liberal arts, the trivium (grammar, rhetoric, logic) and the quadrivium (arithmetic, geometry, astronomy, music). These were considered propaedeutic to sacred learning which is found in the Bible.

How had Greek learning been reduced to these few arts? A contemporary of Cassiodorus, Boethius ("the last of the Romans and the first scholastic") had undertaken to put into Latin the works of Aristotle and Plato, Greek being one of the casualties of the dimming of the lights in Europe. Boethius himself perhaps studied in Alexandria, and thus had lived experience of the last phase of the Athenian school, which was exiled there. Boethius died in AD 524 at the age of 44, having led an active political life as well as the life of a scholar. A layman and Catholic, scion of an old Roman family, he had served Theodoric the Ostrogoth who had become emperor and set up his court in Ravenna. Boethius held various offices in Rome, Theodoric wanting the vestiges of the Roman Empire to continue. The eastern empire had gone its own way and was headquartered in Constantinople. Theodoric accused Boethius of plotting against him on behalf of the eastern empire and sentenced his faithful political servant to death. In Pavia, awaiting execution, Boethius wrote *The Consolation of Philosophy*, the most circulated work after the Bible in the early Middle Ages. In this magnificent work, which alternates poetry and prose, Boethius asked, in effect, how an innocent man like himself should have ended in such a plight.

His great translation project had hardly begun. Boethius left translations of a few works of Aristotle, as well as commentaries on them, the *Categories* and *On Interpretation*, perhaps others. He also wrote a work *On Arithmetic* and another *On Music*. These translations and independent works, closely based on Greek texts, became part of the curriculum in monastic education as outlined by Cassiodorus. Cassiodorus had also worked for Theodoric, but survived the experience, and it is thanks to him that the authenticity of Boethius's theological tractates was established. Thomas Aquinas was to write commentaries on two of those treatises. That the same man could write those treatises and end by writing the *Consolation* caused Dr Johnson to wonder how he could write as *magis philosophus quam Christianus* (as more a philosopher than a Christian). That wonderment points to the central puzzle of the Middle Ages, namely, how men of faith could feel so completely at home in classical pagan thought.

Training in the liberal arts was based on authoritative texts, authorities, and authors (*auctores*). Priscian and Donatus wrote the texts on which the study of grammar was based. Cicero was the authority for rhetoric and Aristotle for logic. These arts, along with those of the quadrivium, worthwhile in themselves, were thought to have the further advantage of facilitating an intelligent reading of Sacred Scripture. Monastic life was summed up in the Benedictine motto, work and pray, *ora et labora*. The monastery was self-sufficient, with its own farms and cattle and butteries, and serfs congregated around it. Other monastic work in addition to that of providing for the necessities of life was the copying of manuscripts.

It is important to know the chancy way in which ancient, and indeed medieval, texts have come down to us. If a monastery was to acquire a text it lacked, a copy of it would have to be made. By the copying and trading of manuscripts, libraries were enlarged. This was done in the writing room, the *scriptorium*, and we have illustrations in which a monk sits in the center of a circle of monks reading a text while those around him write down what he reads. Not surprisingly, no two copies of a work would be exactly alike. Our critical editions are the painstaking result of tracing copies to the originals from which they were made, a pursuit which often ends with a number of manuscripts, no one of which is a copy of the others. The collation of these, and the selection of the best reading, issues eventually in a text which is to some degree the product of modern scholarship but which we read as presumably most akin to the lost original.

Monastic prayer consisted of the common liturgy, the Mass, and the chanting of the hours of the office which provided the schedule of the monastic day. Matins and Lauds were chanted in the early morning hours; Prime, Tierce, Sext and None marked hours on the daytime clock; and at evening Vespers was sung, followed finally by Compline. It was the choir monks, to be distinguished from those who worked in the fields, who were the recipients of the education meant to fit them for their liturgical tasks. The thirteenth-century abbey of Montecassino carried on this centuries-old tradition, and it was into it that the child Thomas was introduced.

Thomas remained at Montecassino from 1230 until 1239, when war flared up and made life in the embattled monastery unsafe. Thomas would retain warm relations with Montecassino all his life. His uncle had been abbot and, as we shall see, that post was dangled before him a few years later. But was Thomas ever a member of the Benedictine Order? He was called an oblate when he arrived, an offering, and there has been speculation that he continued on into membership in the Order, taking the vows of a monk. Since he left Montecassino at the age of 14, this is on the face of it unlikely. In the event, he would become a friar and a mendicant.

3

University of Naples (1239–1244)

From Montecassino, Thomas was sent to Naples and the university founded there in 1224 by the emperor Frederick II. The monastic schools had been complemented later by cathedral schools, founded under the aegis of Charlemagne and his mentor Alcuin. The latter schools flourished as towns and commerce grew and the rural location of most monasteries caused them gradually to lose their hegemony in education. Education was, of course, largely the training of clerics. The monastic school aimed to form members of the community; the cathedral school trained future priests for the bishop around whose chair – *cathedra* – the school formed. Until well into the twelfth century, the curriculum reflected an assumption as to the relationship between secular and sacred learning. Instruction in the rudiments of the arts by the *scholasticus* or schoolmaster, with study of the Bible, prepared the future priest for his ministerial duties.

In the twelfth century, Paris emerged as the European center of education. The left bank of the Seine came to be known as the Latin Quarter because Latin was the lingua franca of the students who came there from all over Europe to study. There was the cathedral school of Notre Dame on the Île de la Cité, an island in the Seine, and on the left bank the houses of study of Benedictines. Saint-Germain des Prés later became engulfed by the city but it was named after the meadows on which it first rose. Nowadays the abbey church stands where city streets cross, looking very urban yet still capable of eliciting from imagination the monastic community that once surrounded it. There was, too, the community of the Augustinian Canons of Saint-Victor where Hugh and Richard and others put their stamp on the thought and spirituality of the twelfth century. And of course Abelard came to Paris, drawn by the magnetism of its intellectual energies. So too John of Salisbury. John conveys something of the excitement of that time in his account of the masters under whom he studied in Paris, the *Paralogicon*. It is sometimes said that the twelfth century is not accorded the importance it deserves because it had the misfortune to be followed by the thirteenth. But this neglect has long since been remedied. As a result, the emergence of the university out of these pre-existing schools where masters plied their trade is less mysterious than it was once considered to be.

But lively as the twelfth century was, in some areas it remained utterly traditional. Thus, in logic, Abelard, hardly the most conformist personality in the Middle Ages, confined his logical teaching to the works that for centuries had constituted the authorities of the discipline: Porphyry, Boethius, and Aristotle. The Problem of Universals which had been bequeathed to the medievals by Porphyry in his *Isagoge* or introduction to the *Categories* was expatiated on by every commentator, beginning with Boethius. Were genera and species figments of the mind or real? If real, were they corporeal or incorporeal? If corporeal, did they nonetheless exist in bodies or elsewhere and apart? Porphyry was thinking of the different positions of Plato and Aristotle, but the medieval commentators knew Plato only later, and in a partial translation of the *Timaeus*, and Aristotle through a few logical works. For all that, these proliferating rival positions on the status of universals, spurred by the study of Augustine and his identification of Plato's Ideas with the divine Ideas, have their charm. Eventually, Abelard wrote a book, the *Dialectica*, which was meant to present logic as such and not as a commentary on authoritative books. Alas, there is little in it that is not in the commentaries and the *auctores* clearly influence the structure and arguments of the work. The transition from *auctor* (author) to *auctoritas* (authority) was an obvious one in this context.

Augustine and the Church Fathers, some Greek as well as Latin, influenced sacred learning, Augustine being accorded the enormous authority he has rightly retained ever since. At the very beginning of the twelfth century, Anselm in a monastery at Bec in Normandy composed a series of absolutely fundamental treatises: *On Truth, On the Fall of the Devil, Proslogion, Monologion*, etc. Augustine is the main influence on him, no doubt, but the power and originality of Anselm's mind rises from these pages. Eventually he would be named archbishop of Canterbury with not altogether happy consequences. A century that began with Anselm would see education become urban and international and competitive. Abelard is always a special case, but his exalted self-estimate was grounded in undoubted genius and a personal flair that made him the stormy petrel of his time. No need to recount his eventually tragic tutoring of Héloïse and their love affair which caused her enraged uncle to unman the tutor. He tells it all in *The Story of My Calamities* and we have as well the letters of Héloïse. After the attack in which he was castrated, Abelard left Paris for monastic life where it would be cruel to say he was a soprano in the choir. Héloïse became a nun and remained fiercely faithful to her erstwhile lover. It was her self-effacing insistence that they not marry so Abelard could continue as a cleric and teacher that led to the tragedy. A cleric was constituted by receiving the tonsure. Abelard was not a priest, however, and when he fell in love with Héloïse and consummated their love, the fruit of their union was a son for whom the wounded Abelard composed moving poems. This episode is often taken to be the emergence of personality in the Middle Ages, but no one can read Anselm without becoming acquainted with his powerful personality. It was the personality asserted rather than the awareness of personality that distinguished Abelard from Anselm.

There was something chaotic as well as vibrant in the competition of twelfth-century masters, although gradually there was a movement toward organization and common standards and the emergence of the university – the *universitas magistrorum et scholarium*, community of masters and students – with a chancellor, at first a diocesan official, and the modeling of the apprenticeship of future masters on that of the guilds. This happened at the dawn of the new century, and soon universities sprang up all across the continent as well as in England, at Oxford and Cambridge. Hence the founding in Naples by Frederick II of his own university, to which the teenage Thomas came.

In Naples, Thomas came into contact with members of the Order founded by St Dominic (1170–1224), a Spaniard who insisted on the theological training of the friars so that they could better preach the word and counter the Albigensian heresy. Thomas found the new Order attractive and at the age of 19, in 1244, he became a Dominican. The presence of the friars, Dominicans and Franciscans, was to lead to controversy in the university, as the secular masters, that is, diocesan priests, resented this invasion of the mendicant friars. This was a controversy in which Thomas himself would become involved, in Paris.

But the transition to the university cannot be fully appreciated without understanding how the hegemony of the traditional liberal arts education was broken by the arrival in Latin translation of hitherto unknown, save by title, works of Aristotle, until eventually the whole Aristotelian corpus, convoyed by Arabic commentaries, altered forever the nature of higher education. The *Nicomachean Ethics*, in partial and then in full translation, became available before the twelfth century had ended, though not in time to influence the remarkable treatise of Abelard, *Know Thyself*, in which the intention with which one acts was stressed almost to the exclusion of what one actually did.

At Naples, Thomas became acquainted for the first time with the excitement generated by the realization that the liberal arts were no longer adequate to contain the scope of secular learning. The new learning was resisted, particularly at Paris, where there was a ban on basing courses on Aristotle that lasted until 1230. Aristotle, and the associated learning from Islamic circles, expanded Thomas's understanding of the range of secular learning, and he found Aristotle almost as attractive as he did the Dominicans. Naples was of course international, and Thomas had an Irish master, Peter, in logic.

When he joined the Dominican Order, Thomas was sent north to complete his studies, but his journey was to be dramatically interrupted.

4

Under House Arrest (1244–1245)

Thomas's family were appalled to find that he had joined the ragtag band of friars called Dominicans – in Latin *Dominicanes*, which was sometimes broken up into *Domini canes*, that is, dogs of the Lord – and were not disposed to acquiesce. Accordingly, while he was journeying north from Naples, he was taken from the band of friars by his brothers and sequestered in a family castle where sense could be talked to him. It was not a clerical vocation that was objected to, but joining so *infra dig* an outfit as the dogs of the Lord. If Thomas wanted a religious life, there was always Montecassino. His mother Theodora wanted Thomas to go there; after all, an uncle had been abbot, and ecclesiastical promotion of a kind that could gladden the family heart was possible there. It is said that Thomas's rejection of this suggestion because of his Dominican allegiance was countered with the proposal that he could enter Montecassino as a Dominican! That a mendicant friar should rule over a rich monastic community is a clear case of ecclesiastical oil and water. After all, the Dominicans and Franciscans were a standing rebuke to the complacency and ease that had crept into the religious life.

Thomas was adamant in his vocation, but for a long year he was kept under what amounted to house arrest during which he is said to have continued to wear the distinctive white-and-black habit of a Dominican friar. As best he could, he tried to live the life of a religious, but there were other occupations as well. His little work *On Modal Propositions* (those propositions involving "possibly" and "necessarily" which modify the way in which the predicate is said of the subject) was written at this time, but its authenticity is disputed.

His mother invoked allies in Rome to influence Thomas, but his brothers had recourse to cruder persuasion. They introduced a woman of easy virtue into Thomas's room, seeking to appeal to the young man's reason through his concupiscence. As the story is told, Thomas snatched a brand from the fire and drove the poor girl from the room. Then, with the charred end of the stick, he traced a cross on the wall and fell on his knees before it. He had passed what his brothers regarded as the supreme test. An angel is said to have appeared to him and tied a cincture around his waist, and from that time Thomas was untroubled by carnal temptation. This as much as his subsequent theology of the angels is the origin of his title as the angelic doctor.

Of course all these stories have been subjected to skeptical doubt by later historians and dismissed as pious myths. But they are power-fully sustained by the oral tradition and figure in the later process of Thomas's canonization. Not every fact is amenable to historical validation or refutation, needless to say, but it is not mere credulity to accept such accounts at face value, as mountains of sober research attest. Of course only Thomas could be the source for the episode with the prostitute and Thomas did not lie – in either sense of the term.

Eventually his family became convinced of Thomas's fidelity to his vocation and he was allowed to rejoin the friars and continue north-ward for the completion of his education.

5

Cologne and Albert the Great
(1245–1248)

Biographers dispute whether Thomas went to Paris before going to the Dominican studium at Cologne, where he studied under a giant of the fledgling Order, the German Albert. There is no doubt that Albert himself was previously a master at Paris, where he commented on works of Aristotle, and it is not impossible that Thomas first came under his tutelage there before accompanying his master to Cologne with the founding of the Dominican studium there. In any case, the two were together in Cologne and it is there, under Albert, that Thomas's remarkable grasp of the writings of Aristotle was consolidated. Albert would author a paraphrase of the complete corpus of Aristotle and at Cologne lectured on the *Nicomachean Ethics*. His commentary would be edited by his pupil, Thomas, and it is interesting to compare Albert's commentary with the much later one Thomas himself would compose at Paris. Thomas found his mentor too heavily indebted to the Arabic commentators and his own exposition is aimed at releasing Aristotle from distorting interpretations.

It was at Cologne that Thomas's taciturnity was noted, leading his fellow students to dub him the Dumb Ox, the latter part of the epithet referring perhaps to the young friar's avoirdupois. Thomas's girth seems solidly attested to, unaffected by the meager diet of a friar and the many taxing journeys that he took. And it was Albert who retorted to Thomas's nickname with his fellow students by predicting that the bellowing of this ox would be heard all over Europe. Bellowing does not seem the apt adjective for the chaste and calm style of Thomas's writings, but the foretelling of his influence was borne out.

6

Student at Paris (1252–1256)

Albert founded a faculty of theology at Cologne in 1245, where Thomas studied under him, then became his assistant. But in 1252 he was sent to Paris, it being the most distinguished center of university education in Christendom. The friars had a house there, the Convent of St James, named after the street on which it stood, which in turn was named for the route to the great shrine of the apostle James at Compostela in Spain. We must now get a sense of the structure of university education at Paris.

The university was composed of faculties, masters and their students, and there were four such faculties. The faculty of arts was the point of entry, where the students began at the age that Thomas had gone to Naples, in their early teens. When the Master of Arts was gained, the student became eligible for one of the advanced faculties, theology, medicine, or law. The name of the Faculty of Arts indicates that it was originally seen as a continuation of the liberal arts tradition, but the influx of Aristotle in Latin translations required an expansion of the concept of secular learning. After all, where among the traditional arts was one to locate such a work as Aristotle's *Physics*, or his *Metaphysics*, *Politics*, and *Ethics*? It couldn't be done. But if Aristotle was resisted, this was not simply because his writings made untenable the notion that the seven liberal arts were an adequate summation of secular leaning. The far more important question turned on the compatibility of Aristotle with Christian faith.

Universities were, after all, Catholic institutions. The University of Paris had received its charter from the pope. Masters and students were all clerics, believing Christians, whose attitude toward an author whose doctrines might seem to conflict with the truths of faith could scarcely be nonchalant. As $-x = x$ is false, if the faith taught X and the philosopher (Aristotle became the eponymous philosopher in the thirteenth century) taught ~X, clearly the philosopher was in error if the faith was true. The other possibility, that the philosopher teaching something in conflict with the faith was right and the faith false would not of course have been a live option.

If, from the beginning of the university, Aristotle represented at least a possible problem, this problem was to be exacerbated by the rise of so-called Latin Averroism (discussed on pages 20–3), since it flared up just before Thomas's second stint as a regent master at Paris and he was in the center of the fray.

The master of arts was earned at about the age of 19 or 20 and then, for such a one as Thomas, the long training in theology began. There were, in effect, two tracks. First, the biblical. The fledgling theologian listened to lectures on books of the Old and New Testament for some years and then became an assistant to the master, giving a cursory reading of the text before the master settled down to his magisterial exposition. By stages, the student was advanced into ever more responsible involvement in the teaching of neophytes until he became himself a master of Sacred Scripture. The second track was based on the *Sentences* of Peter Lombard, a twelfth-century master who became eventually bishop of Paris. In four large books, Peter had offered a summary of Christian doctrine which turned on St Augustine's distinction between *res* and *signum*. The divisions of the work were called distinctions. Those of Book One consisted of: the mystery of the Trinity (distinctions 1 and 2); God's knowledge of creatures, whether God is cause of himself, and allied questions of generation within the Trinity (distinctions 5–7); on such attributes of God as truth, unchangeableness, and simplicity (8); the distinction between the persons of the Trinity (9–10); the Holy Spirit (10–18); equality in the Trinity (19–20); the names of the persons (21); how God can be named (22); the meaning of person (23); and of such terms as one, three, many, as applied to persons of the Trinity (24–25); what is proper to each person (26–28); things said relatively of God (29); and temporally (30); how is the Son equal to the Father (31); the Father and Son vis-à-vis the Holy Spirit (32); things said of the divine essence and of the divine persons (33–34); God's foreknowledge, and so on, there being 48 distinctions in the first book. Mastery of the *Sentences* was exhibited by a commentary on those four books, so that among the writings of a master will always be found his commentary on the *Sentences*, and so it is with Thomas.

Thomas's method was to begin with an outline of the distinction which was followed by the treatment of questions raised by it, questions often divided into sub-questions. A question was handled by mimicking, in effect, the procedure in public disputations. A suggested answer to the question posed was confronted with a number of objections, followed by the solution, usually a defense of the proposed answer and then a response to the objections to that answer. This is the method Thomas would follow in the questions of the *Summa Theologiae*.

This demanding course of study took the student into his early thirties when he would be formally recognized as a master of theology. After that, in the case of a mendicant, he might go off to some other university or to a house of studies of his Order, and function as a master. The Dominican Order had two chairs in theology at Paris, and Thomas was appointed to a three-year term in one of them after he became a master.

There are several works of Thomas which date from his student years, including *On Being and Essence* and *On the Principles of Nature*. His *Commentary on the Sentences* is placed in 1252–1254.

7

First Paris Professorship (1256–1259)

Bonaventure, the great Franciscan, completed his work for the master of theology at the same time as Thomas, but because of the opposition of the secular masters the two men were not welcomed into the magisterial body until a papal intervention forced their acceptance. The tasks of the master of theology were summed up in three Latin infinitives, *legere. disputare, praedicare*: to lecture, to dispute, to preach. Thomas had been ordained a priest in 1250 or 1251 in Cologne. His lectures were given in the Dominican Convent and his sermons were university sermons, learned discourses, not unlike his inaugural lecture when he was installed as a master, in which he spoke of the relationships between the various books of the Bible. (Late in his life, in Naples, he preached popular sermons on the Commandments, on the Lord's Prayer, and the Ave Maria.) Disputations were of two kinds, Disputed Questions and Quodlibetal Questions. In Thomas's time, such disputes were dominated by the masters; later the Quodlibetals became more student affairs.

The master posted a thesis he was prepared to defend some days before the event, then the other masters and students came ready with objections to the thesis. An assistant would give an initial response – part of the apprenticeship – and then came the magisterial response. Afterward, the master was required to deliver a written version to the university stationery so that copies could be ordered by those able to afford the vellum and copying fees. We have an enormous number of disputed questions of Thomas, two large volumes in modern printed editions, the one *On Truth* comprising some 29 constituent questions which make up the first of the volumes. Scholars dispute whether these represent 29 different occasions, unlikely since disputations were held twice in the liturgical year and Thomas was a reigning master at Paris for only six years in all. As it happens, some disputed questions were held during the decade-long Italian period between Thomas's two magisterial stints at Paris. Others of his disputed questions are *On the Power of God, On the Soul, On*

Spiritual Creatures, On the Union of the Incarnate Word, On Evil, On Virtue in General, On Charity, On Fraternal Correction, On Hope, and *On the Cardinal Virtues.*

In their written form, the question is posed and an answer suggested, followed by numerous objections to it, then appeals to authority on behalf of the proposed answer, followed by argument(s) in favor of the answer and then a response to each of the objections raised. In their written form, the disputed question is not a transcript of the occasion, but it captures the dialectic of the event. Such disputes complemented the close textual expositions of the lectures on Scripture and on Peter Lombard.

Quodlibetal questions were free-for-alls where the master made himself available to discuss anything that might be thrown at him. Written versions of these were distributed, and the volume of Thomas's *Quodlibetal Questions* conveys the range and variety of such occasions, very picayune points jostling with more substantive issues.

If the demands on the student of theology were onerous, those on the regent master were even more so. Nor was Thomas's production limited to writings that arose more or less directly out of his magisterial functions. Thomas's expositions of Boethius's *De Hebdomadibus* and *On the Trinity* (the commentary breaks off in chapter 2 of the work but is by no means negligible, as we shall see in Part II, page 67ff.) date from this period. In 1259 he began what would be his only completed summary of theology, the *Summa contra Gentiles* (it was not finished until 1265). This work is noteworthy because it devotes so much space to what we can know of God by reason alone.

8

Italian Interlude (1259–1268)

It was the Dominican practice to have one of the masters of the Order teach for three years at Paris, thereby acquiring the éclat of the premier university, and then going off to houses of study of the

Order to teach those not fortunate enough to study at Paris itself, though perhaps that lay in the future for some of the young friars. Thus it was that Thomas, in 1259, returned to Italy where for nearly a decade he taught in a variety of places: in Naples; then, from 1261, in Orvieto where the court of Pope Urban IV was located; and, from 1265, in Rome at Santa Sabina, as well as in Viterbo where Pope Clement IV had his court.

One of the achievements of this period was the completion of the *Summa contra Gentiles*, of which Thomas's own manuscript has been preserved. The third book is in the Ambrosiana in Milan, and the day that Father Angelo Paredi put those precious pages into my hands is among the memorable events of my life. A feature of Thomas's manuscripts is the obvious haste with which they were written, in shorthand Latin, in a scrawl which led to calling a text of Thomas's *litera inintelligibilis*, unreadable writing. Eventually he would be assigned secretaries, among them Reginald of Piperno, who took down Thomas's dictation, a process which doubtless increased his productivity. (Reginald is the source of much of our knowledge of Thomas the man.) Weisheipl points out that Thomas was the first member of the Roman Province of the Dominican Order to become a master of theology in Paris, and this undoubted prestige led to his appointment as preacher general of his province. We must not forget that Thomas was an active member of his Order, attending all the annual provincial meetings held during his sojourn in Italy, listed and dated as follows by Weisheipl: Orvieto (1261), Perugia (1262), Rome (1263), Viterbo (1264), Anagni (1265), Todi (1266), Lucca (1267), and Viterbo again (1268). Attendance involved a good deal of traveling around the peninsula. It was in 1261 that Thomas was assigned as lecturer at the convent at Orvieto, and during his four years there he formed a close friendship with Urban IV.

During his stay in Italy, Thomas became aware of the new translations and revisions of Aristotle made by his fellow Dominican, William of Moerbeke. The study of Aristotle is an unbroken feature of Thomas's intellectual life, a study only tangentially connected with his duties as a master of theology. The nomadic papal court is an indication that hostilities with Frederick, and later Manfred, made Rome less than safe for the pontiff, so that the presence of the papal court in towns north of Rome may be seen as a kind of exile. One of the most impressive and self-effacing works of Thomas is the *Catena Aurea* he composed at the behest of Urban IV. This is a commentary on the four Gospels, which strings together in a golden chain expositions drawn from the great teachers of Christendom, the Church Fathers, both Greek and Latin.

Early in the Italian period Thomas commented on a work of an enigmatic figure who styled himself Denis the Areopagite, a convert of St Paul's. Since Denis lived in the sixth century, either he was very long-lived or he was employing a nom de plume. He was a Neopla-tonist and Thomas's interest in him attests to the fact that Thomas's Aristotelianism was assimilative rather than exclusive. Thomas himself did not realize that he was dealing with an author who came to be known as "Pseudo-Dionysius," but that is by the by. His com-mentary on the work called *On the Divine Names* is one of several in which Thomas moved with great sympathy into an approach which might seem to be antithetical to his own Aristotelian convic-tions. His reading of the text is at once sympathetic and such that it is seen as complementary rather than in opposition to what he had learned from Aristotle. Thomas's commentary on the work known as *The Book on the Causes*, based on the Neoplatonist Proclus's *Elements of Theology* – a provenance Thomas was the first to see – is also indicative of the assimilative rather than confrontational nature of Thomas's mind.

It has been mentioned that Thomas throughout his career steeped himself in the writings of Aristotle. When he went to Rome in 1265 to teach at the Dominican studium at Santa Sabina, his Aris-totelianism was to manifest itself in a remarkable new way. Probably in 1268, in Rome, he began the series of close commentaries on the Aristotelian treatises which was to occupy him for the rest of his short life. His commentary on Aristotle's *On the Soul* was at least begun in Rome, and perhaps completed when he returned to Paris into a tumultuous situation during which, as we will see, there was an urgent need for the kind of close reading of Aristotle that Thomas's commentaries on the Stagirite exhibit.

It was also in Rome that he began what would be his theological masterpiece in three parts, the *Summa Theologiae*, the first part of which was completed before 1268. Another aspect of Thomas's genius was exhibited in the Office he composed for the newly insti-tuted feast of Corpus Christi. The Eucharistic hymns he wrote for this Office continue to be sung throughout the world.

9

Second Paris Period (1269–1272)

It was highly unusual, indeed unprecedented at the time, for anyone to be appointed a second time as a Dominican regent master in Paris, but doubtless Thomas's presence was wanted because of the controversy that had flared up around what is called variously Latin Averroism or Heterodox Aristotelianism. This was a controversy over the relationship of Aristotle to the faith. We have seen that there were misgivings about the compatibility of Aristotelian philosophy and Christian faith from the earliest years of the university. Thomas's writings during his first stint as regent master and since displayed his confidence that Aristotle was more an ally than an enemy to Christian theology. Others were not so sure. Thomas's great contemporary, Bonaventure, who was elected master general of the Franciscan Order, became increasingly wary of Aristotle's influence and with the rise of Latin Averroism this hardened into hostility. The problem can be summarized in the so-called errors of Aristotle.

1   Aristotle taught that the world had always existed, that it was in that sense eternal, a teaching clearly contradictory to the Christian belief, based on Genesis, that "in the beginning" God created heaven and earth. Either the world had a beginning or it did not. It is a matter of Christian faith that it had a beginning. Therefore the philosophical teaching that the world is eternal is false.

2   Aristotle was said to deny personal immortality, his proof of the separability of intellect from matter in On the Soul taken to be that there is an incorruptible intellect that is the cause of the thinking of human beings but is not a capacity of their souls. But Christianity is unintelligible without the belief in the soul's continued existence after death, your soul and mine. Once more, a contradiction.

3   Aristotle seems to teach that it would be demeaning for God to have knowledge of the world. But for the Christian, God's

eye is on the sparrow and he knows the number of hairs on our heads. Either God knows the world or he does not. One of these views must be false.

The second "error" is due to Averroes's reading of *On the Soul*. The Latin Averroists or Heterodox Aristotelians were masters in the faculty of arts to whom the infamous "two truth" theory is attributed. That is, what they seemed to be saying is that something can be true in philosophy and false in theology, and vice versa. As Aristotelians, as philosophers, they accepted the cogency of positions which were in conflict with their presumed Christian beliefs. No matter. The eternity of the world is a philosophical truth, its non-eternity is a truth of faith.

Thomas's response to this was twofold. First, he simply rejects as absurd and incoherent the view that both sides of a contradiction can be true. This is to violate the most fundamental law of thinking, the principle of contradiction, $-(p. - p)$. Moreover, it is impious to suggest that God presents for our acceptance as true something we know to be false.

Second, he insists that Aristotle did not teach 2 and 3, as a close reading of his texts shows, and, while he taught 1, which is false, its falsity could not have been known by Aristotle or anyone else on the basis of natural reasoning but is only established as false on the basis of revelation. Thomas wrote a little book, *On the Eternity of the World*, to make this point. He dealt with the second supposed error in another little work, *On There Being Only One Intellect*, in which he argues that the Averroistic interpretation of *On the Soul* cannot be reconciled with the text. So too he holds that God's supposed non-knowing of the world is a bad reading of the *Metaphysics*.

Thomas's position was complicated by the fact that anti-Aristotelians tended to lump him together with the Latin Averroists, finding Thomas's own predilection for Aristotle suspicious. In 1270, a condemnation of a number of theses of an Aristotelian provenance created an official hostility to Aristotle. (In 1277, after the death of Thomas, another condemnation of 219 theses contained several taught by Thomas.) The urgency of the situation cannot be overstated. If the spirit of the condemnations had prevailed, the university would have turned its back on the enormous philosophical achievement of Aristotle and even more seriously called into question the assumption that faith and reason are complementary, not inimical, to one another. What Aristotle taught was not true because he taught it but represented what the human mind, unaided by faith, could know. That Thomas understood what was at stake is clear from the short works just cited and even more by the sequence of commentaries on the Aristotelian treatises he produced, some dozen in the course of perhaps five years, and at a time when he was fulfilling the onerous duties of a regent master as well as continuing work on his *Summa Theologiae*. When we realize that the Aristotelian commentaries were a species of moonlighting, not part of Thomas's task as a master of theology, their very existence is a testimony to how concerned Thomas was to protect the range of reason.

In them, Thomas may be seen as doing the work of a master in the arts faculty as it should be done. Thomas, like many others, learned much from the commentaries of Averroes and Avicenna, which were translated along with the texts of Aristotle. But we see, in his earliest writings, a wariness about the Arabic readings of Aristotle; this increases during his career, so that the severe treatment of Averroes during this second Parisian period does not surprise. It has often been noted that in his commentary on Aristotle's *On the Soul*, the first of his commentaries, Thomas shows no sign of responding to a contemporary problem. The criticisms of the Avicennian and Averroistic interpretations of certain texts are familiar ones, often encountered in Thomas's earlier writings. The crisis of Latin Averroism upped the ante, as it were. No longer was it a simple question of a dubious reading of a text, to be confronted as such. Now the young men whom Ferdinand Van Steenberghen preferred to call heterodox Aristotelians were undermining the most fundamental assumption of the university, that what can be known and what is believed can never really contradict one another. In all periods of the history of philosophy there have been those who say blithely that they are willing to accept incoherence and to live with contradictory beliefs. But even the statement of this willingness becomes mere gibberish if its contradictory has equal status. Thomas was coming to the defense of the reasonableness of the faith, but equally he was coming to the defense of reason and saving philosophy from the philosophers.

A word more about what Thomas said about the eternity of the world. Of course, either the world is eternal or it is not. And of course the believer believes that it was created in time, in the beginning. It is false to hold that the world is eternal. Thus far, this is simply an application of the principle of contradiction. A proposition and its contradictory cannot be simultaneously true. Christians *believe* that one of the contradictories is true and so the other is false. But could one in this case settle the matter on the basis of reason? Can we know one way or the other if the world is eternal? Thomas maintains that this is undecidable on the basis of reason alone. This means that Aristotle could not have known the truth that the world is not eternal. But didn't Aristotle think he knew the world is eternal? Thomas finds his arguments only probable, but of course if Aristotle thought they were apodictic, he was wrong.

This may give some indication of the subtlety and care with which Thomas approached discussions of the relationship between faith and reason, and of course it indicates his conviction that Aristotle is the best guide to philosophical truth, deserving the benefit of the doubt when difficulties arise. Here is the list of the Aristotelian works on which he commented: *On the Soul*; *On Sense and the Sensed Object*; *Physics*; *Meteorology*; *On Interpretation* (incomplete); *Posterior Analytics*; *Nicomachean Ethics*; *Politics* (incomplete); *Metaphysics*; *On the Heavens* (incomplete); *On Generation and Corruption* (incomplete). That's eleven. He also composed the *Tabula Ethicorum*, an ethical dictionary based on Aristotle.

Work on the *Summa Theologiae* continued during this tumultuous time. Thomas moved on to the Second Part, the moral part, which he subdivided, treating the more general moral principles in the First Part of the Second Part – *Prima Secundae* – and then the virtues in the Second Part of the Second Part, *Secunda Secundae* (theological, cardinal, acquired and infused, the gifts, etc.). It is an astonishing synthesis of the whole patristic tradition and the philosophical. The Third Part is devoted to Christ, the Incarnate Word, and the sacraments. Question 90 is the last Thomas wrote, but it does not complete the plan of the *Summa* as Thomas had conceived it. Because the work was well planned, others later cannibalized Thomas's commentary on Peter Lombard, cast it into the form of the later work, and completed the *Summa* in what is called the Supplement.

Some of Thomas's disputed questions date from this second Parisian period, as do some of the quodlibetal questions, proof enough that Thomas was fulfilling the ordinary tasks of a master of theology despite the distraction of the Latin Averroist controversy. He lectured on Matthew's Gospel, and a written version has come down to us. We also have his commentary on John which dates from this period *On the Perfection of the Spiritual Life* and *Against Those Opposing Joining Religious Orders* date from this same period, attesting to the fact that the animosity which had delayed Thomas's reception into the faculty of theology had not gone away. Thomas was ever a stout defender of his vocation and of the fittingness for a friar to teach. He also wrote *On Separate Substances* at this time. And there are responses to requests that came from all over, on subjects as diverse as taking interest on money lent to the treatment of Jews. Correspondents would send him lists of questions, 6, 30, 36, 43, and Thomas would discuss them one by one.

Thomas's output during these three years in Paris seems scarcely credible. Of course he wrote by dictation but that is far from explaining the quantity, the range, and the depth of his writings at this time. He was at his zenith, no doubt, at the height of his powers and indefatigable. As for the great crisis of the time, one might say that Thomas established the complementarity of faith and reason as much by example as by explicit argument. Chesterton was right to see Thomas's defense of reason as a watershed of European history.

Not that Thomas's views triumphed in the short term. As has been mentioned, he was tarred in the minds of some with the same brush as the Latin Averroists, his inordinate love of Aristotle being to the detriment – so went the charge – of the faith. In the short term, Thomas's opponents won, most of them Franciscans. The condemnation of 1277 clearly put Thomas in the target area. This was after his death, of course. Then Franciscans began to make compilations of what they took to be Thomas's distortions. Dominicans responded. The two mendicant Orders who did so much to reform the Church throughout the thirteenth century ended it as intellectual opponents.

10

Naples (1272–1274)

Thomas could have been forgiven if he was glad to get out of Paris and return to Italy. He went by way of Florence to Naples, the origin of his Dominican vocation, to teach in the Dominican house there. Within a year something strange occurred. On December 6, 1273, Thomas decided to stop writing. Some biographers conjecture that he had a kind of mental breakdown. But it was a mystical experience that silenced Thomas. After what he had seen, he told Reginald, everything he had written seemed mere straw. He could not bring himself to complete the *Summa*. Nonetheless, when he was asked to attend a council called at Lyon, he set off on December 6, 1273. He was not to reach his destination; he was not to get out of Italy. He was injured in an accident on the way, a branch overhanging the road banging his head and knocking him to the ground, perhaps from the back of a donkey he was riding. Weisheipl conjectures that a clot on the brain formed as the result of this and grew larger every day. Thomas could not go on and stopped at Maenza, at the castle of a niece, Francesca. The Cistercian abbey of Fossanova was in the vicinity and when Thomas's condition worsened, he was transferred to the monastery. It was there, on March 7, 1274, that he died.

Dante gave credence to the story that Thomas was assassinated by Charles of Anjou, fearing that at the council Thomas would be named cardinal and as a future pope would be a formidable enemy. Here in Dorothy Sayers's translation are the lines.

> Charles came to Italy; to make amends
> He slaughtered Conradin; and after this
> Packed Thomas off to heaven, to make amends.
> *Purgatorio*, xx, 57–69

False, of course, so why mention it? The *Divine Comedy* is set in the year 1300, a quarter-century after the death of Thomas and Bonaventure. That these and other Parisian masters figure prominently in Dante's great poem attests to the influence of that university and the lasting impact of the outcome of its quarrels. Bonaventure was created cardinal. Reginald of Piperno, Thomas's companion, predicted this, and that Thomas too would get a red hat. Given Thomas's rejection of ecclesiastical promotion, one wonders if he would have accepted. A future pope? Who knows? In any case, it is mere conjecture. Thomas assured Reginald he would go on exactly as he was. And so he did. He died a simple friar, in a Cistercian monastery, in the fifth decade of his life.

In Part III something of what happened next is described.

SELECTED FURTHER READING

Cacopardo, Rocco. *Se veramente Tommaso d'Aquino, come scrisse Dante, fu assassinato*. Rome: Rizzoli, 1995.

Chesterton, G. K. *Saint Thomas Aquinas*. New York: Sheed & Ward, 1954.

Dondaine, Antoine. *Secrétaires de Saint Thomas*. Rome: Commissio Leonina, 1956.

Ferrua, Angelica. *Thomae Aquinatis Vitae Fontes Praecipuae*. Alba: Edizioni Domenicane, 1968.

Maritain, Jacques. *St Thomas Aquinas*. New York: Meridian Books, 1958.

O'Meara, Thomas F. *Thomas Aquinas: Theologian*. Notre Dame and London: University of Notre Dame Press, 1997.

Pieper, Josef. *The Silence of St Thomas*. South Bend: St Augustine Press, 1999.

Torrell, J. P. *Saint Thomas Aquinas*. Washington: Catholic University of America Press, 1999.

Weisheipl, James A. *Friar Thomas d'Aquino*. New York: Doubleday, 1974.

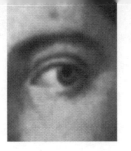

— PART II —

In Pursuit of Wisdom

The *Summa Theologiae* is Thomas Aquinas's masterpiece. Most of the other titles in his collected writings are also manifestly theological. On the assumption that theology and philosophy differ, this poses an obvious question: how can Thomas be a key philosophical thinker if he is a theologian?

In recent times, the received opinion among professional philosophers has been that religious faith cannot withstand the scrutiny of reason. But theology is a reflection on religious faith which assumes the truth of what is believed. Theology, consequently, is regarded by the professional philosopher as just as suspect as the faith whose truth it assumes.

This attitude, whatever else one might say of it, presupposes a distinction between philosophy and theology, probably reducible to a distinction between sense and nonsense. Thomas Aquinas engaged in philosophy as well as theology and distinguished between the two in a clear and persuasive way. The aim of the distinction, however, was the reverse of our contemporary one – rather than to dismiss theology, he sought to recognize two different kinds of discourse.

11

Theology Presupposes Philosophy

A first thing to notice about Thomas's comparison of theology and philosophy is that he clearly supposes that the study of the former presupposes that one has already studied the latter. That is, only someone trained in philosophy could profitably take up the study of theology. That this is his view is clear from the first question asked in the *Summa Theologiae*: "Is any teaching beyond that of the philosophical disciplines necessary?" The *Summa* was written for theological neophytes and proposes to give them milk to drink before starting them on a meat diet, but these theological beginners are assumed to be proficient in philosophy. If they were beginners in philosophy as well as in theology, that opening question could have no meaning for them. It would not present a difficulty to be resolved. And of course – we shall return to this – the method of the *Summa* is the serial surmounting of difficulties.

The Sacred Doctrine which is beyond the philosophical disciplines is conveyed to us in Holy Scripture, the Word of God, which is accepted as true on the authority of the one revealing. By contrast, the philosophical disciplines are anchored in truths that anyone can know. Without religious faith revealed truths will not function for everyone as truths, and faith is gratuitous, a gift, not something owing to us as if it were standard human equipment. It is otherwise with philosophy. Its starting points or principles are available to all. Philosophy can become obscure, no doubt, but it must not start that way. Its initial task is to reflect on and clarify the truths that no one with standard cognitive equipment could fail to know. It is these truths that make up the principles of philosophy.

If in recent times any distinction between philosophy and theology (as presupposing the truth of revelation) is made in order to put the latter out of business, Thomas's distinction between the two is meant to distinguish two kinds of discourse that one and the same human mind can engage in. But, as has been pointed out, that human mind cannot engage in theological discourse until and unless it has become reasonably proficient in philosophical discourse. This does not mean that religious faith presupposes philosophizing. Theological discourse is something some believers engage in and, on Thomas's understanding of it, in doing so they will bring to bear on the truths of faith the methods and doctrines they have acquired from the study of philosophy.

In summary, we can say that philosophical discourse will take its rise from truths which are in the common domain. Theological discourse takes as its principles truths which have been revealed and are accepted as such on the basis of the gift of faith. However logically flawless a theological argument might be, it can be a truth-carrier for its addressee only if its principles are accepted as true. And this acceptance requires the gift of faith. Philosophical discourse is based on sweet reason and begins where everybody already is by dint of being a human being.

12

The Quest of Philosophy

There is thus no reason in principle why Thomas Aquinas could not be both philosopher and theologian. Indeed, on his own view, he could not have become the second if he had not already become the first. What did Thomas take philosophy to be?

We have seen that Thomas lived at a time when the writings of Aristotle, previously known only in a few titles, came rapidly and completely into the West in Latin translation. The accompanying accounts and interpretations, Muslim and Jewish, presented other problems as well, but in Aristotle, *the* philosopher, the Christian believer had a clinical specimen of what the world looked like to one uninfluenced by religious faith. Revelation is over and above what man's natural endowments can attain; Aristotle thus becomes the privileged representative of what man can know using only his natural powers. A truism of the relation between these two orders is that the supernatural presupposes and does not destroy the natural. The avidity with which Christian believers sought and studied the texts of Aristotle can best be understood in this wider context.

The ambience of faith within which the believer engages in philosophy has seemed to some to entail that the believer cannot truly engage in philosophy at all. This criticism is rooted in quite modern notions of how philosophy begins. Unlike the assumptions given above – that the philosopher begins with truths everyone already knows – since Descartes the initial task of the philosopher has been taken to be the rinsing from his mind of all prior knowledge claims. Various methods were devised to carry this out, such as methodic doubt, and the suggestion is that philosophizing is presupposition-less. The philosopher ideally is uninfluenced by his upbringing and culture; he is an isolated mind, and little else, to which somehow questions occur.

Despite the continuing uncritical acceptance of this fantastic picture of the philosopher, it has been shown again and again to be impossible of realization. Of course, the only reason why one would seek to realize it is because he accepts the scarcely less fantastic assumption that everything one thought one knew prior to formal philosophizing may turn out to be false. For our purposes, it is enough to point out that many of the claims that Thomas could not be a real philosopher because he has all those religious beliefs are grounded on a notion of real philosophy that has no foundation.

Presuppositionless philosophizing is a chimera*

"All men by nature desire to know." This is the opening sentence of Aristotle's *Metaphysics*. On the face of it, this may seem a trifle sanguine. Surely there are one or two, some perhaps among our relatives, whose desire for knowledge is difficult to discern. Fortunately, Aristotle glosses his opening generalization. As if to allay our initial doubt, he follows that opening sentence with, "A sign of this is the delight we take in the senses, especially the sense of sight." Who does not delight in taking a look? The senses are essential to our getting around in the world – "Look out!" is more frequently relevant than "Look!" – but sometimes just looking is sufficiently delightful to us, as shopkeepers will ruefully attest.

*   That this does not relativize philosophizing, making arguments merely a function of one's presuppositions, will be discussed below.

Aristotle continues in this disarming way to help us see the truth of his opening sentence. He moves from external to internal senses – memory and imagination – to experience. What is being underscored is that capacities and activities we share with other animals in us are the prelude to something more. Experience, the holding together of memories of similar events, paves the way for art, illustrated by medicine and teaching. Anyone can attain truths about the world on their own, but it would be a heavy burden if each were required to invent the wheel. The dependence of the young on the old is not stressed in these chapters, doubtless because it is so obvious. The cognitive capacities we have not only function on their own, so to speak, they can be guided by those who have been there before and can speed the process.

We have here the ground of the Aristotelian claim that art imitates nature. This is not in the first instance an aesthetic principle: it is found in the *Physics* before it is used in the *Poetics*. Our natural ability to learn on our own is presupposed by the teacher; it is that natural process he or she will artfully seek to guide.

Art differs from mere experience in that art knows why something works; experience knows only that it does. The midwife will do what she does on the basis of her experience of Mrs Brown and Mrs White and Mrs Black and all the others, some remembered similarity prompting her to act now as she does. To have the art is to know why something has the effect it does. It knows the cause. No wonder one who has art is thought wiser than one with mere experience. She can teach us, not merely apprentice us.

The distinction between looking out and just looking adumbrates the distinction between the practical and the theoretical, knowledge sought for a further purpose and knowledge sought for its own sake. "Art" is first used in a way that does not distinguish between the knowledge of the why that is aimed at making and that which is sought for its own sake. The latter is illustrated by mathematics and such knowledge is linked with leisure – Aristotle says that it was the priestly caste in Egypt that had the leisure to devote to mathematical inquiry. The term "geometry" suggests surveying, something quite practical, but as later codified by Euclid, about a century after Aristotle, geometry is the quintessential instance of asking for the why of a theorem, proving it, and giving the reason why it is so. That is what knowledge is, *episteme*, science, knowing *why* and not just *that* something is so, seeking this for its own sake.

Aristotle is now ready to provide us with an explanation of the term "philosophy." It is the love of wisdom, the quest of wisdom. One having art rather than mere experience was said to be wise. Wisdom in the full sense is knowledge, not simply of the why or cause of some truth, but knowledge of the highest and most comprehensive truths. Having anchored the quest in the most common and widespread human activities, Aristotle now stresses that the goal takes one far beyond. The wise person will know all things it is possible to know, difficult things, and knowing the cause he will be able to teach us.

Like Plato, Aristotle locates the origin of philosophy in wonder. We see something happen, for example an eclipse, and wonder what is going on, why that is happening. Wonder is an index of ignorance, of not understanding. The pursuit of knowledge then would seem to be the elimination of wonder. In some sense this is true, but there is wonder and wonder. The ultimate aim of philosophizing may seem the presumptuous desire to have the knowledge only God could have. Perhaps this hubris will be punished, as the poets suggest. "Bards tell many a lie," Aristotle responds, and then adds that the ultimate aim of philosophy is indeed a divine science. A theology. It is divine in two ways. "For the science which it would be most meet for God to have is a divine science, and so is any science that deals with divine objects; and this science alone has both these qualities; for God is thought to be among the causes of all things and to be a first principle, and such a science either God alone can have, or God above all others. All the other sciences are more necessary than this, but none is better."

13

Theoretical and Practical

The first supporting example for the claim that we all desire to know is the delight we take in seeing – even when we have nothing beyond just looking in mind. This is a foreshadowing of a distinction which provides another way of arranging and relating the various philosophical disciplines, the distinction between the theoretical or speculative, on the one hand, and the practical, on the other.

A text to which Thomas invariably refers when he discusses this matter is chapter 10 of Book Three of *On the Soul*. "Both of these then are capable of originating local movement, thought and appetite: thought, that is, which calculates means to an end, i.e. practical thought (it differs from speculative thought in the character of its end)." We use our minds in different ways depending on different purposes. When we take thought against a sea of troubles and seek by opposing to end them, our thinking aims at results beyond the realm of thought. Squinting down the fairway from the tee, the golfer plans how he will play the hole. Having done so, he selects a club, takes his stance, waggles and shifts and then, alas, slices the ball into the rough. Not at all what he had in mind. Often our thinking aims at a result beyond thinking and our execution of the plan is faulty. The standard case, of course, is the successful doing of what we thought about doing.

But not all thinking is like that. A repentant golfer, revisiting the scene of his misspent life, might stand on the tee and looking outward simply take pleasure in the green expanse before him, the twitter of birds, the hum of insects, the sun warm on his arms. He just looks. That he might write a sonnet about it later for *Golf Digest* was not the aim of this contemplative moment. There are intellectual pursuits which are undertaken for their own sake, in order to know, period. The joys of plane geometry are self-contained; little Orville learns how to prove a theorem, and does so. What's the good of doing so? Just knowing the properties of a circle. Some knowledge is its own reward.

It is not just our pragmatic age that can find it difficult to admit speculative or theoretical knowledge in this sense. Natural science has been so linked to technology that inquiry seems always, however remotely, aimed at producing some benefit to mankind, a harmless cigarette, say. Pure science may seem a chimera. As the opening panorama of the *Metaphysics* makes clear, there is a priority of the practical in our lives. Our senses are principally aimed at helping us get around in the world safely and our minds are first put to the acquisition of food, shelter, and safety. It is no accident that art and medicine are discussed in the passage before science or that the acquisition of leisure – that is, being able to take for granted the practical order – released priests to the study of mathematics, for its own sake.

The theoretical and practical are first distinguished in terms of their aims or ends. We are using our minds practically when thought aims at some goal beyond thinking – building a house, or crossing the street safely. There are other criteria for this distinction. Some people might delight in reading cookbooks or instructions on how to build a boat, but never cook or build a boat. What they are thinking about is ordered to something other than thinking, but their aim is merely to fantasize. Astronomy deals with something we cannot do anything about even if we wanted to. The cosmos is just there and coming to know about it is the only cognitive stance we can take toward it. The object of knowledge may be such that it could not be put to any practical purpose. You will object that knowledge of the stars has since time immemorial been useful for navigation. (Thales, the very first philosopher, is said to have written a book on celestial navigation.) True enough but only incidentally so. The stars in their courses are what they are independently of any contingent value knowledge of them may have for us. Geometry can be put to practical use, but the truths of geometry are what they are before and independently of this.

Of course, people can think about objects that could be made by us but in much the same way they think of natural objects. *Jane's Ships* has the look of a work in natural science, describing, comparing, and classifying vessels as the entomologist might bugs. The aim of *Jane's* is not to help you build your own aircraft carrier. Cookbooks, on the other hand, give instructions which when followed issue in such things as shrimp fried rice. And so does that one book Chesterton said he would choose to have with him on a desert island, *How to Build a Boat*.

Those are the three criteria Thomas proposes for assessing whether an instance of knowledge is theoretical or practical: end, object, method. This rather lengthy discussion will stand us in good stead later when we turn to Thomas's moral thought. For now it provides the framework on which to array the philosophical disciplines. Philosophical sciences are either theoretical or practical, that is, deal with things we can make or do or with things we simply know. The three theoretical or speculative philosophical sciences are natural philosophy, mathematics, and metaphysics. There are three practical sciences as well, Thomas holds: ethics, economics, politics.

This schema does not mention logic, and a dispute raged during the Hellenistic period as to whether or not logic was a part of philosophy. We will return to this on page 42.

14

The Order of Learning

Thomas lays out the best way to pursue the philosophical sciences in the prologue to his commentary on the *Book of Causes*, a work of Neoplatonic origin. As Thomas was the first to show, it is made up of selections from Proclus's *Elements of Theology*. For Thomas, the work he is about to comment on is clearly an exercise in the culminating philosophical effort, wisdom, or theology. Before settling down to his task, Thomas locates the work in the wider scheme of inquiry,

Thomas's prologue is in many ways a reprise of those opening chapters of Aristotle's *Metaphysics*. Thomas eventually wrote a commentary on the *Metaphysics*, in which he dwells on the opening chapters we have been summarizing. Here, in the preface to his commentary on the *Book of Causes*, he refers to the Aristotelian text, making explicit what of course is implicit in the quest as Aristotle describes it. We begin with what is easy for us to know, the things of sense, the world around us, and we proceed only gradually to knowledge of the ultimate causes of all things, the kind of knowledge that was called divine in several senses. The things we come ultimately to know are difficult and remote from the beginnings of our knowledge. So let us state it explicitly. What we first and most easily know is on the bottom in the scale of things and what we eventually and with difficulty come to know about, the ultimate causes, are on the top of the ontological scale. What is first in our knowing is least in being; what is ultimate and difficult in our knowing is the most perfect in being. Thomas recalls a simile of Aristotle's. Our intellect is, with respect to the ontologically perfect, like the eye of a nightbird with respect to the sun.

Against this background, Thomas gives the following pedagogical advice:

> Hence the chief aim of philosophers was to consider all things in order to arrive at knowledge of first causes. That is why they placed knowledge of first causes last, in the final stage of life, and began first with

logic which treats the mode of the sciences, went on next to mathematics which even children are capable of learning; third, to natural philosophy which requires time for experience, fourth to moral philosophy of which the young are not suitable students, and finally they turned to divine science which considers the first causes of being.

Now we see what those "philosophical disciplines" mentioned in the opening discussion of the *Summa Theologiae* are: logic, mathematics, natural science, moral philosophy, and divine science or theology.

15

The Two Theologies

We began by discussing the relation between philosophy and theology. Now we seem to have two sorts of theology, one of which is regarded as the culmination of the philosophical quest, identical with wisdom defined as knowledge of all things in their first causes. In short, there seems to be a philosophical theology, a theology of the philosophers, as well as a theology which is distinguished from any and all of the philosophical disciplines.

Nowadays, among professional philosophers, there is almost as much disinterest in philosophical theology as there is in the discourse based on revealed truths. In its first phases, modern philosophy, even while it was a conscious and often contemptuous alternative to Aristotelian or Scholastic philosophy, devoted a good deal of attention to proving the existence of God. Such proofs arrived at rather exiguous conceptions of God and, with time, they ceased to be part of the philosopher's job description until finally, as we said at the outset, it is as if professional philosophers are agreed that talk about and attempts to prove the existence of God are nonsense.

There are notable and noble exceptions to this among our philosophical contemporaries, but philosophical theists often seem to be in the philosophical dock, required to prove themselves innocent of one epistemological faux pas or another.

But back to the two theologies. Consider this passage from Thomas's earlier summary, the *Summa contra Gentiles*:

> There is a twofold kind of truth in the things we say about God. For some things are true of God which exceed the capacity of human reason, such that God is three and one. But there are some to which even natural reason can attain, such as that God exists, that he is one, and the like, which even philosophers have demonstratively proved of God, led by the light of natural reason. (I, 3)

What I have translated blandly as "things we say about God" would be more accurately rendered, "that we confess about God." Writing as a theologian, Thomas is thinking of the faith we profess, as in the Creed, and it is the truths about God that show up there that lead him to make the above distinction. It may strike us as paradoxical at first, but for the believer it is a matter of faith that God can be known apart from faith, that is, in the light of natural reason. For the Catholic, since the nineteenth-century Vatican I, this is *de fide*. That human beings can apart from faith know God is taken to be the clear meaning of the scriptural text that from time immemorial – and in Vatican I – is invoked to show this. Of course the paradoxical element here is that one invokes a scriptural passage in order to hold that one need not appeal to scripture or faith in order to know that God exists.

Writing to the Romans, St Paul remarks that men can from the things that are made come to knowledge of the invisible things of God. Paul is not just making a philosophical point, of course, he is about to chide the Romans for their misbehavior and, since they are not Christians, he must do so in terms of merely human or natural capacities. The idea is that one who knows that God exists, and realizes his or her own creaturely dependence on God, has a powerful incentive not to behave as the pagan Romans did. Thomas, in commenting on this passage, invokes the Neoplatonist thought to be Denis the Areopagite, one of Paul's converts.

> From such creatures man can know God in three ways, as Denis says in *On the divine names*. First, *by way of causality*. Since such creatures are defective and mutable they must be dependent on something immobile and perfect. And in this way it can be known that God is.
>
> Second *by way of excellence*. Things are not reduced to the first principle as to their proper univocal cause, as a father is the univocal cause of his child, but to their universal cause that far exceeds them. Thus God is known to be beyond all other things.

Third, *by way of negation*. For if there is such a cause, nothing found in creatures can belong to him, anymore than celestial bodies can be called light or heavy, warm or cold [in the same sense as terrestrial bodies]. In this way we call God immobile and infinite and the like. (*Super Epistolam ad Romanos Lectura*, ed. R. Cai, OP, Marietti, 1953, n. 115)

Thomas adds that this threefold knowledge is had by the natural light of reason.

These are matters to which we will return later (page 88ff.), following the order of discussion Thomas has laid down. What we have said about the theology that is opposed to the philosophical disciplines and about the theology which is the culminating philosophical discipline is for the moment mere information. Of course, philosophizing does not properly begin with topics that make up its end, its ultimate quest. But on the level of information, it is well to have an overview, however obscure, of the terrain over which we are about to pass. The beginner in philosophy takes all this on the word of his teacher, presumably wise, who has reached the goal and is helping the learner to get there. Such trust or faith is human and must eventually give way to knowledge.

But I want to add a few more preliminary things in the next chapter before we begin at the beginning and go on from there.

16

The Four Orders

Aristotle remarks in those opening chapters of the *Metaphysics* that the wise man, knowing the ultimate causes, should order or lead, and not be ordered or led. *Sapientis est ordinare*, as this is succinctly put in Latin. When Thomas opens his commentary on Aristotle's *Nicomachean Ethics*, he recalls this maxim and reflects on it. There is a twofold order, he first notes, insofar as the parts of something are ordered or related to one another but the thing as a whole is also ordered to some further end. The elements of an army are ordered to one another but the whole army is ordered to victory in battle. That being said, since ordering requires reason, Thomas next relates order to reason in four ways.

> There is one order that reason does not establish but only beholds, such is the order of things in nature. There is a second order that reason establishes in its own act of consideration, for example, when it arranges its concepts among themselves, and the signs of concepts as well, because words express the meanings of the concepts. There is a third order that reason in deliberating establishes in the operations of the will. There is a fourth order that reason in planning establishes in the external things which it causes, such as a chest and a house. (*Nic. Ethic. I*, Lect. 1, n. 1)

We have here an alternative approach to the constitutive sciences of philosophy that occurs in the text advising us of the proper order in learning them. There is an order we discover but do not construct, the natural order, the cosmos. There is an order we construct in knowing natural things, one piggyback on our knowledge of them. Thus animal is called a genus and man a species. "Animal" and "man" signify things that are; *genus* signifies a relation that attaches to knowing them, that of being predicable of many specifically different things. *Species* attached to man means that "man" is predicable of many numerically different things. These second-order words are logical words, signifying logical not real relations. The third order is the moral order, the rational direction of our will in choosing and desiring. The fourth order is the order our practical reason imposes on the things it makes, and this is the realm of art.

We will have to say more of each of these as we go on, but it is convenient to have such a text before us now when we are just getting acquainted with Thomas's thought and seeking an initial familiarity with it. Is this just the learning of a jargon? Thomas, like Aristotle, would have been shocked to hear that anyone thought he was proposing some arbitrary way of thinking or talking, call it the Thomistic way. The desire for originality in philosophy – of making personal claims to this item of knowledge or that – arguably present here and there from the beginning of the history of philosophy, has assumed epidemic proportions in recent centuries. Early or late, such personalizing of the quest for truth claims authority from some private experience, for example, being swept up into the heavens in the case of Parmenides and a dream in the case of Descartes. Thomas at any rate was innocent of it. That being the case we will be particularly eager to know why his way of thinking and talking, however initially odd and arbitrary we might find it, is taken to be the natural way of the human mind.

17

The Logical Order

In the text from the prologue to the *Book of Causes*, logic was said to teach the mode of the sciences. That is, it deals with the kind of thinking we must do if the result is to be knowledge, what Aristotle called *episteme* and Thomas called *scientia*, that is, knowledge in the strong sense of the term. And what is that? We can say we know something in this strong sense when what we know is not only true but is also necessary, that is, it could not be otherwise.

Ideas aren't true, only affirmations or denials are, that is, when we attribute something to something, minimally, such as "*S* is *P*." Logic is chiefly concerned with discourse providing reasons for thinking that such a combination as "*S* is *P*" is true. Of course, it could be true simply on the face of it. If I say a whole is greater than any of its parts – e.g. there is more to you than your feet – or if I say that two things like a third thing are like one another – e.g. you two are alike in that you both have your mother's hair – our assent would not be withheld. Knowing what is meant by "whole" and "part" or "alike" seems to suffice for knowing that such claims are true. Truths of this kind are important for the analysis of what scientific discourse is because they are presupposed by such discourse.

These truths, ones that gain assent straightaway, are called immediate to distinguish them from the truths which are the chief concern of the analysis of knowledge in the strong sense. These are truths which are seen to be so because they derive from other truths, are mediated by them. That is, they exemplify a syllogism. The syllogism is one of the great achievements of logic, however disparaged it sometimes is today. Such disparagement often stems from the realization that there are other kinds of argument than syllogism, so that it would be simplistic to say all reasoning is syllogistic. That is easy to concede, but not perhaps that they are of equal importance in analyzing knowledge in the strong sense.

A syllogism is a sequence in which something is seen to be so because others things are so. The thing that comes to be known is the conclusion and what is set before it, from which it follows, are the premisses. The premisses contain that which links or mediates between the elements of the conclusion, that is, "S is P." Formally, we can express this as:

M is P
S is M
S is P.

It is because P is said of M and M is said of S that P is said of S. The formal logic of the syllogism is a lovely subject in itself. The mediating or middle term might occur as in the example just given, the first figure or shape of the syllogism. But the middle term might be the subject of both premisses, or the predicate of both premisses, and these ground what are called the figures of the syllogism, which classically are taken to be three, the fourth possible arrangement undercutting rather than exemplifying the sequence.

All that – one finds it in Aristotle's *Prior Analytics* – is presupposed to the analysis of the syllogistic discourse which yields knowledge in the strong sense. We are struck in reading that analysis – in the *Posterior Analytics* – by the way in which mathematical examples abound, nor is this an accident. Once all the requirements and characteristics of apodictic or scientific discourse are seen, the question must arise as to what could possibly satisfy this demanding ideal. An obvious answer is the sort of arguments with which we are familiar from plane geometry. The proof that the sum of the internal angles of a plane triangle equal 180 degrees is one that gladdened our youthful hearts and rightly gave us a sense that we were in touch with a necessary truth. It is because of what a plane triangle is that this property necessarily belongs to it. No one who recalls the joys of plane geometry will regard that as a tautology, that is, as merely "S is S." Something we will have to keep in mind in what follows is that what Thomas refers to as the philosophical disciplines are called that with reference to the demanding criteria of apodictic discourse.

But let us conclude this glance at logic with a text from Thomas's prologue to his commentary on the *Posterior Analytics*, a text which puts before us a cascade of modes of argument which fall away in increasing degrees from the scientific syllogism. Thomas leads up to this by reference to those logical works of the Organon that are presupposed by knowledge in the strong sense. Since the syllogism is made up of propositions, the logic of propositions is presupposed, what Aristotle discusses in *On Interpretation*. And, since propositions are made up of terms whose meanings must be known – "Define your terms!" – what Aristotle discusses in the *Categories* is even more fundamentally presupposed, the logic of definition. Apodictic discourse follows on these, but we must take note of the fact that not all argument is scientific or apodictic. Reasoning, discourse, is not always necessary. Since logic is an art and art imitates nature, the fact that some things in nature come about necessarily, others for the most part, and yet others rarely, is an analog to the modes of discourse.

In apodictic discourse we have a rational process which yields necessity, where truth cannot fail and certitude results. But there is also discourse which arrives at a conclusion expressive of what is usually though not necessarily the case. And there is discourse which has only the look of producing truth.

> That part of logic which yields the first is called Judicative, judgment being what gives the certitude of knowledge. Because a certain judgment of effects can only be had when they are resolved into first principles, this part of logic is called Analytics, that is, resolutive. Such certitude consequent on resolution or analysis is due either to the form of syllogism alone, discussed in the *Prior Analytics*, which deals with the syllogism as such, or due also to the matter, propositions which are per se and necessary, discussed in the *Posterior Analytics*, which deals with demonstrative syllogism. (*Prooemium*, n. 6)

There is also the logic of discovery, which does not always yield certitude. What is discovered must be judged and often we judge that what we have come up with is not certain. Then, instead of knowledge in the strong sense, science, we have opinion, based on the probability of the propositions from which it follows. It is as if our task is to answer the question symbolized by $p \vee {\sim}p$. In knowledge in the strong sense, the mind settles on p to the total and necessary exclusion of ${\sim}p$. In opinion, the mind opts for p but, in the expressive phrase *cum formidine alterius*, in the awareness that ${\sim}p$ may be true.

Aristotle's *Topics* are said to deal with such arguments, a doctrine that is called dialectical.

When an argument merely causes us to suspect that *p* is true, we nonetheless opt for it because the argument is persuasive, appealing to our emotions as well as our mind. Aristotle's *Rhetoric* is concerned with such arguments. Thomas then speaks of poetic argument, in which our opting for *p* as opposed to –*p* follows on how something is presented. "The *Poetics* is concerned with this, for it is the mark of the poet that he commends the virtuous by some fitting representation."

Finally, Aristotle's *Sophistical Refutations* is concerned with the recognition of fallacious reasoning, discourse which only seems to lead to a conclusion.

Let this suffice as a sketch of the nature and scope of logic as Thomas learned it from Aristotle. In explaining *On Interpretation*, Thomas mentions sentences which are not expressive of truth: questions, prayers, various performative utterances such as the words of consecration in the Mass – "This is my body; this is my blood" – and then says they are not relevant to the task at hand. There is no suggestion that there is something bogus or defective about such utterances; somewhat similarly, in acknowledging the various kinds of discourse, his attention is on the apodictic. It is knowledge in the strong sense that is the desired objective. But the other modes of discourse have their legitimate place in our lives.

18

Our Natural Way of Knowing

The opening chapters of the *Metaphysics* make clear the primacy of the senses in human knowledge. Our ideas are abstractions or generalizations from the singular things our senses grasp. We grasp things as kinds and our concepts are progressively more adequate to what things are as learning progresses. Intellectually, we know singular sensible things as instances of a universal, as animal, as man, or as apple or orange. Knowledge of sensible singulars comes first, with the grasp of them by our senses – we see this, hear that, feel the other thing, all singulars – and then mentally sort them into this kind of thing, that kind of thing, the other kind of thing.

> This is something we can experience in ourselves, namely that when one tries to understand something, he forms certain images for himself by way of examples, the understanding of which he seeks. So too when we wish someone else to understand we provide examples from which he can form images to be understood. (*ST* 1.84.7)

If our intellectual knowledge always involves universals, and if things as they exist are singular, it may seem that our knowing them is the necessary distortion of the things known. They are singular; we know them universally. But this is to know them otherwise than as they are. And that seems the very definition of false knowledge. The way in which things exist is not the way in which we understand them. Here is Thomas's answer:

> When the intellect which understands things otherwise than as they are is said to be false, this is true if 'otherwise' refers to the thing understood. For the intellect is indeed false when it understands a thing to be other than it is. For example, were it to abstract the nature of rock from matter and understand it to be without matter, as Plato held. But the objection does not hold if 'otherwise' refers to the one understanding. It is without falsehood that the way a person understands should differ from the mode of existence of thing understood. What is understood is in the thinker immaterially following the mode of intellect, not materially, in the manner of the material thing. (*ST* 1.85.1.1m)

It is just here that modern philosophy has diverged from the epistemological realism that characterizes the thought of Thomas Aquinas. In one way or another, since Descartes, the assumption has been that we know things as we know them and this precludes our knowing them as they actually are. Descartes rummaged around in the inventory of his concepts, wondering if any was such that it required him to say that it had some counterpart outside his mind. In the case of the idea of God he found this to be necessary. But the thing to notice now, for our purposes, is his assumption that things as they are known, that is, in our mind, are the primary objects of thinking. With Kant of course it became definitional that our way of knowing, the forms of sensibility and the categories of understanding, generate phenomena, that is, things as they are known, always to be distinguished from noumena, the unknowable things in themselves. The resolution we have just cited was not formulated by Thomas with any notion of the lengths later philosophers would retreat from the robust sense that what we know is the things that are. That the mode of our knowing them differs from the mode of their existing is the explanation not the denial that our knowledge is of the things themselves. The notion that we first know our knowing, and that this renders problematical our knowledge of things, is pandemic in modern philosophy. Of course, it would be Pickwickian to attempt to prove that what we first know is the things that are. What is needed is to show the incoherence to which a denial of this has led. This may not be the work of a summer's day, nor does such refutation cause relativists to fold up their tents like the Arabs and as silently steal away. But such refutations, which occupied so many pages of Plato and Aristotle, are in any case chiefly aimed at protecting the tyro from taking the fatal step into bad subjectivity.

The connatural and proper object of the human mind is the quiddity, essence or nature of the sensible thing. The nature or essence can be considered in three ways, in itself, in matter, or in the mind. Consider the following:

1   Man is rational.
2   Man is a species.
3   Man is seated.

That the predicates of these sentences differ may be seen by trying certain inferences. Man is a species; Socrates is a man; Socrates is a species. Clearly something has gone wrong here. If by species we mean what is predicated of numerically different things, that clearly cannot be said of Socrates – maybe the name "Socrates" but not the husband of Xanthippe.

So too if we try: Man is seated; Socrates is a man; Socrates is seated. That might turn out to be true, happen to be true, Socrates might be the one whose being seated justifies our saying "Man is seated." But seated men rise and remain men, suggesting that the connection between being a man and being seated is incidental.

As opposed to what? Man is rational; Socrates is a man; Socrates is rational. This works because we have in mind the nature as such, the whatness, and what belongs to it per se, as such. Thomas's phrase for this is *natura absolute considerata*: the nature considered without reference to the incidental. It is incidental to what it is to be a man that this or that man is seated. To be seated does not enter into our account of what a man is. That does not mean that it is false to say a man is seated, when he is, but only that for him to be seated is not an essential mark of being human. Of course we could construct a long disjunction – is seated or standing or lying down or ... – but this would emphasize the incidental character of the components rather than overcome it.

As being seated is incidental to human nature, so too is being a species. "To be said of many numerically different things" is not true of human nature taken as such; this is something that is true of it *as we know it*, that is, universally. Universals – species, genus, difference, property – name logical relations which attach to but do not constitute the nature. Our intellectual knowledge of sensible things is forever universal, but that is our way of knowing them, not a constitutive feature of them. If it were, we could have concluded above that Socrates is a species.

The "problem of universals" kept thinkers busy during the early Middle Ages, but tended to fade into the background with the influx of Greek and Arab texts. For all that, a correct understanding of universals is crucial if we are to avoid the equation of intellectual knowledge with false knowledge. The fact that it is I who know whenever I know does not entail that autobiographical remarks become part and parcel of accounts of what I know. Somewhat similarly, the fact that in knowing the natures of things we concentrate on what is essential, and that relations of predicability and universality attach incidentally to these natures, does not entail that universality – or singularity – enters into our account of these natures. That is the sense of Thomas's phrase *natura absolute considerata* – considering the nature without mentioning its singular conditions or the relations it takes on as we know it.

19

Matter and Form

Apart from Parmenides, perhaps, the Greeks were agreed that there is a world to be understood and that the most obvious thing about it is change. It is made up of things which come to be as the result of a change (are generated), change constantly while they are (change place, qualities, quantity) until that dramatic and final change when they simply cease to be (corrupt). To call them *physical objects* is simply to say that, *phusis* deriving from change. Calling them *natural* has the same effect, being born functioning metaphorically for all change, whether of living or non-living things, a metaphor also present in *phuein*. Navigators and farmers and fishermen and lovers in a meadow have many causes to wonder at what is going on in the world, and wonder is said to be the beginning of philosophy. We ask why something is happening because we don't get it, and when we do, our wonder is assuaged and our ignorance replaced with knowledge.

Should problems just be taken up piecemeal, allocated by occupation or region? Later, some encyclopedist could compile all the results and call it *De rerum natura*. But the compilation would indeed be a pile. Moreover, this way of proceeding is not really appropriate to us. Do particular problems come first?

Of the assumptions of Thomas Aquinas's approach to the natural or physical world, one of the most surprising to us, perhaps, is that we first know things in the most general and universal way, and then gradually over time come to greater and greater specificity as to the kinds of things. We have been prepared for this by things said earlier, but its elevation into the most fundamental methodological rule for the study of nature can, as I say, surprise. Why not start with the elements, the ultimate building blocks, and see how things are variously made up of them? Something like that is received opinion now, and Thomas's procedure cuts athwart it.

What is at issue is what is the most natural way for us to seek knowledge of the singular changeable things around us. The question is, what is the most natural *way* for us to know these singulars? Intellectual knowledge is always of kinds, always involves universals; the suggestion is that we begin with the most universal and shared characteristics of sensible things, and then progress to the notes that divide them.

The analysis of physical objects begins with (a) concrete examples of them, and (b) what can truly be said of any of them. The example Thomas finds in the text of the *Physics* where all this is said is: man becomes musical. It might be translated as: man becomes educated. A beautifully ambiguous example. It is natural for human persons to learn and acquire arts, so the example can stand for any and every change. Perhaps Aristotle thought the realm of art provides for us a good avenue into the natural. In any case, that is the example that will have to carry the tremendous load of yielding characteristics true of each and every physical object just as such.

There are two major steps in the analysis. First, the change that is spoken of in "man becomes musical" can be expressed in several ways:

1　Man becomes musical.
2　The non-musical becomes musical.
3　The non-musical man becomes musical.

If one of these is true, they all are, and each is prompted by noticing Ellen practicing her scales on her violin. A child becomes musical; one who is not musical becomes musical; a non-musical child becomes musical. That this is boringly obvious is just what we want; we are on the threshold, the obvious can be mentioned, it's all right.

Second, the form of all these expressions of the same change is "*A* becomes *B*." But sometimes we say, "From *A*, *B* comes to be." What's the point? This. Imagine converting the above list into the second form of expression.

1′　From man, the musical comes to be.
2′　From the non-musical, the musical comes to be.
3′　From the non-musical man, the musical comes to be.

We now have six different ways of expressing our example of change. All of these variations have this point: doesn't 1′ suggest something odd? The form "From *A*, *B* comes to be" suggests that when you have *B*, *A* no longer is. But of course once Ellen has mastered the violin she is still the lovely little girl she was before. She hasn't ceased to be. On this basis, we are able to distinguish *the grammatical subject of the expression of a change* from *the subject of the change*.

By "subject of the change" we mean: that to which the change is attributed and which survives the change. In the variations given above, the only grammatical subject of which this can be said is man.

The subject of the change acquires a characteristic it does not have prior to the change. Minimally, then, the most sweeping yet true thing we can say of any change is that it involves three things: a subject, a lack, and a new characteristic.

It is the alteration of the example that led to a terminology being fashioned whose career continues to this day. Imagine someone whittling wood – another example of art. The wood takes on a shape or form it did not previously have. It is here that we have the basis for speaking of the subject of a change as its wood, *hyle*, matter; and the characteristic it takes on as shape or form, *morphe*. The fact that the matter lacks the form prior to the change is dubbed *steresis*, privation.

20

Things that Come to Be as the Result of a Change

In giving a schema of the proper order in which the philosophical disciplines should be learned, Thomas put logic first. But learning implies a teacher and the teacher knows all kinds of things we hope he will enable us to understand. *Oportet addiscentem credere*, Aristotle said in Latin translation, and of course in learning we put ourselves in others' hands, trust them at least for the nonce, take their word for this or that before we know it to be true. Given man's social nature, it can be said that to learn and be taught is our natural way. For all that, we should have to distinguish learning from discovery, since the former presupposes the latter.

The analogy Thomas likes here is that between a wound or illness being cured by nature and its being cured by medicine. The medical art imitates nature in the sense that it seeks to bring about more surely and quickly what nature does. A person is capable of arriving at knowledge about the world by himself but it is quicker and easier if he can be brought to knowledge by one who already has it. Those who first discover things, good luck aside, are accounted to have stronger minds, but it would be an impossible burden if even such a mind had to discover everything for itself.

All this is prelude to saying that, apart from the order of learning and teaching, it would be odd to say that men first discovered logic. Knowledge begins with the effort to understand the things around us, the things our senses grasp, and whose natures or kinds our mind seeks to understand. The effort to understand such things will provide us with a vocabulary which will be progressively extended to things more difficult to know, and ultimately to talk about God. The explanatory vocabulary of St Thomas, like that of his mentor Aristotle, is remarkably small. As we shall see, it is possible to track the extensions of terms first applied to the analysis of physical objects and see how later and more difficult doctrines are dependent on those we are about to look at.

The analysis of change yields the view that every change involves a subject or matter, a privation in the subject of the form acquired as a result of the change. The product of change, accordingly, is a compound of matter and form, of the subject and the acquired characteristic. The example analyzed is of the subject's coming to be such-and-such. When the child learns how to play a musical instrument, the child comes to be, in a certain respect, as a musician. The same would be said of change of place and change in quantity, as in growth. Can the analysis be applied to the coming into being of the subject as such, a substantial, as opposed to the incidental change of the subject, which is an autonomous thing or substance?

The assumptions of this further move are two: that there are substances, and that substances come to be and pass away. Neither of these is in need of proof. That there are basic units in the world is a given; so too is the fact of their coming into and passing out of being. If every change involves matter, form, and privation, we must understand each of these terms differently than we do in the case of incidental change. If substances come to be, a subject is involved, but the subject in this case cannot itself be a substance. If it were, the form acquired would not constitute the substance as this kind of substance, but indicate an incidental property of it. Aristotle suggests that the subject of substantial change is known on an analogy with that of incidental change. That is, the subject is known and spoken of with respect to subject in the usual sense, that is, as substance. The fact of substantial change requires a subject but one that is not itself a substance. The form acquired is one that constitutes the substance as the kind of substance it is. The subject of a substantial change, its matter, is called prime matter to indicate that it is a principle of substance and not itself a substance. The form acquired is called a substantial form.

It should be noted that "form" in its primary sense of shape, the external contours of a substance, refers to quality. Already, when the new place the substance acquires in locomotion is called its form, there is an extension of meaning of the term. To understand this usage, one must see the similarity to yet difference from the acquisition of a new shape. The acquisition of quantity may result in a change of shape or form in the primary sense, but to call 180 pounds a new form of the substance involves an extension of the meaning of the term. Thus, the need to recognize a plurality of senses of the key term does not arise for the first time in the analysis of substantial change, although here the extension is more radical. In all these cases, of course, the key terms tell us something generically true and do not specify the form or matter or privation in a way that would make them appropriate to a specific kind of change. That is, the result of locomotion will be described differently in terms of specific kinds of locomotion.

When he sets about the analysis we have been recapitulating, Aristotle uses a variety of examples to illustrate the way in which our knowledge of things moves through a series of progressively more specific designations. Children call all men father and all women mother. In doing so, they are using "father" and "mother" in a generic way. When the child calls an older male a daddy, he does not mean that the man has children of his own, but only that he is like the man they have been taught to call daddy. What precisely earns their male parent the appellation daddy is as yet unknown to the child. Thus, in speaking of individual persons, the child first knows and designates them generically, and only gradually comes to the specific knowledge which limits the application of father, at least in the sense of "my father."

Aristotle also uses the example of something seen afar off. At first one knows only that there is something on the horizon. Then, as the knower moves toward the object, or vice versa, more specific knowledge is gained: it is moving itself, it is alive, it is an animal, it is a human, it is daddy. This is the model for our progressive knowledge of physical objects. Accordingly, the initial use of "matter" and "form" has the sweep of the original use of "daddy" or, in the second example, of "something" or "a thing." The analysis is true, but true on such a level of generality that it calls for more and more specification.

It should not be thought that the more specific designations are deduced from the more generic. Thomas distinguishes between what he calls "the order of determination" (*ordo determinandi*) and "the order of demonstration" (*ordo demonstrandi*). Demonstrations are possible at high levels of designating the subject, but the further specifications of the subject result from experience and induction.

21

The Parmenidean Problem

In the *Physics*, Aristotle takes obvious pleasure in showing that his analysis enables him to solve the dilemma which Parmenides had thrown as a wrench into the development of natural science. Strictly speaking, what Parmenides has to say does not fall to natural science as such, since it amounts to a denial of the assumptions of that science, and a science does not have the resources to prove the ultimate principles with which it begins. We have, then, an excursion into a higher science, one that comes to be called metaphysics.

Parmenides argued that change and multiplicity are logically impossible because we cannot differentiate between things, and change involves the unacceptable assumption that being becomes non-being and non-being becomes being. He takes this to involve the contradiction that since being becomes non-being, being is non-being. Aristotle's solution to this relies on a readily available distinction that is anything but technical. If I say that the golfer golfs, I am attributing to him an activity that is his just insofar as he is a golfer. If, on the other hand, I should say that the professor golfs, I am prepared to agree that he does not do this insofar as he is a professor. In this imperfect world, golfing is not part of the job description of the professor. Rather, it just happens that a golfer is also a professor and of course vice versa. In short, an activity can be attributed to something either as such, per se, or incidentally, *per accidens*.

Parmenides's problem arises from noticing that in speaking of a change we say that something becomes what it is not, that is, we seem to say that being becomes non-being, that is, being = non-being. Aristotle says that Parmenides is quite right, if what he says is understood as per se predication, but not if it is understood as incidental predication.

> Being becomes non-being.
> Non-being becomes being.

Understood per se these amount to the nonsense that bothers Parmenides. Water warming in the sun is an example of a natural change.

> Cold becomes warm.
> Non-warm becomes warm.

Does cold become identical with warmth as the result of the change; does the lack of warmth become identical with warmth as the result of the change? If so, Parmenides's point carried, and it looks as if any effort at natural science is grounded in an illusion.

What Parmenides has left out of account is the subject of the change. It is not the previous quality cold that becomes warm, but the subject that was cold. It is not the subject's previous lack of warmth that becomes warmth as the result of the change, but the subject that lacked warmth. That to which the change is attributed per se is the subject, not its privation or previous condition. By attributing change per se to privation and previous form, Parmenides arrived at a contradiction. The recognition of the subject and that the novelty arises only incidentally from the privation and previous form, insofar as they inhere in the subject, dissolves the Parmenidean problem.

It is just here that another terminological landmark occurs. That to which the change is attributed only incidentally is not such that it can come to be the result of the change. Warmth cannot become non-warmth; warmth cannot become cold. It is the subject that *can* become warm, it is the subject that *can* cease to be cold. The subject thus has the potentiality to acquire the new form and, when it has, it actually has that form. The subject or matter is thus said to be or to have potentially the form that it acquires as the result of the change and actually to have that which is its after the change has occurred. This distinction between can and is, between the potential and the actual, arises easily from ordinary talk. Like the couple matter/form, potency/act have a long career ahead of them.

22

The Sequel

The work of Aristotle called *Physics* represents the initial and most general stage of natural philosophy. It continues by discussing the most common characteristics of physical things. Despite this high level of generality, a number of extremely important truths are established, definitions secured and, in its final books, a demonstration offered which makes it clear that to be material or physical, changeable, is not identical with to be. With that demonstration of the Prime Mover the way is opened for the development of the culminating task of philosophy called variously by Aristotle wisdom or first philosophy – first in the sense of most important, not of course chronologically first – or, in the title later given to the work in which this task is undertaken, metaphysics. Let us at least enumerate the achievements that occur between the initial analysis we have been retailing and the enormously important proof with which the *Physics* end.

The subject matter of natural philosophy is the physical object of which we can now say that it is composed of matter and form. Any science seeks to understand its subject matter by assigning the causes why it is so and why it does the things it does. Thus Aristotle goes on to define nature – the first principle of motion and rest in that in which it is found per se and not incidentally – and the causes of natural things. These are four in number. The constituents of the natural things are explanatory of it: a natural thing has a material cause and a formal cause. The changes we began by analyzing do not just occur; they are brought about. There must be some agent or efficient cause of water's passage from being potentially to actually warm. This process is understood in terms of the goal at which it aims and in which it terminates. The final cause is for Thomas as it was for Aristotle the cause of the other three causes, the reason for the sake of which the agent acts and a new form comes to inhere in the matter or subject. A complete understanding of the physical object will appeal to all four causes.

If change characterizes physical objects, we must ask what precisely motion is. There are few achievements of Aristotle more fundamental than his definition of motion, which is all but unique in not introducing a synonym of motion in defining it. Potentiality and actuality are the key to the definition, which will strike us initially as obscure until its meaning dawns upon us. Motion is the act of a being in potency insofar as it is in potency. Prior to motion the thing actually is what it is and potentially is what terminates the change. Once the change has occurred, the subject or matter actually has the new form. Motion is what takes place between those two terms. The first element of the definition – the act of a being in potency – would characterize the subject prior to the occurrence of the change. The being as actual characterizes it as the term. In order to catch the arrow in flight, as it were, we speak of the thing in motion as in act but remaining in potency to further act. The definition enables one to handle Zeno's paradoxes, according to which the moving thing is understood as actually wherever it is, period.

Place – the first container of the contained – and time, the number of motion according to the before and after, provide further landmark definitions in this initial effort to understand physical objects.

It may seem irresponsible simply to list these definitions without spending time on their analysis. But our purpose in gesturing at the sequel of natural philosophy is to draw attention to the way in which later analyses and definitions rely on those already made, carrying over the vocabulary while assigning new and connected meanings to recurrent terms. In natural philosophy, indeed, in philosophy in all its amplitude, this practice provides an Ariadne's thread meant to connect the later and more sophisticated discussions to earlier and more fundamental ones. The label for this is analogy, and we shall be returning to it in chapter 31.

23

The Prime Mover

Motion is the act of the moved thing, not of the moving thing, as is clear from the definition. Nonetheless, the physical mover in moving is moved, though not of course in the same sense that it is a mover. I place my hand on a cool surface and sensation involves, but is not identical with, the altered temperature of my hand: it cools. But in cooling my hand, the surface in its turn is warmed. Every physical mover is also a moved thing, though these two things are true of it in different respects. We are now in a position to sketch the proof of a first unmoved mover.

The proof itself can be given succinctly as follows:

Whatever is moved is moved by another.
There cannot be an infinite series of moved movers.
There must be a first unmoved mover.

This is the first of the five proofs – the *quinque viae* – offered by Thomas in the *Summa Theologiae*. Often that statement of it is thought to be cogent simply on the basis of the premises, and of course in a sense this is true. What is not true is that these premises are self-evidently true. Apart from the preceding analyses and arguments in the *Physics*, the proof would be unintelligible. Thomas writes the *Summa Theologiae*, as we have seen, for beginners in theology who are however adepts in philosophy. The proof as given in the *Summa* is meant to remind them of the hard-won achievement with which the *Physics* ends. Earlier, when he gave the proof from motion in the *Summa contra Gentiles*, Thomas went to some pains to provide the presuppositions of the truth of its premises.

If we had world enough and time we should analyze the proof of the Prime Mover in detail. Over the centuries it has been subjected to much criticism and any adequate defense of it would have to respond to those criticisms. We are not writing a book on that proof, of course, and we are going to have to avail ourselves of the same latitude we presumed in simply stating the definitions which stud the middle books of the *Physics*. In his youthful work *The Principles of Nature*, St Thomas wrote what amounts to a compendium of Aristotle's *Physics*, much as his other youthful work, *On Being and Essence*, can be read as a summary of *Metaphysics*. I mention these works to indicate that, early in his career, Thomas assimilated and embraced the Aristotelian doctrine that we have been sketching.

24

The Soul

Because of their level of generality, the things established in the first stage of natural philosophy are true of all physical things. Of course, physical things differ among themselves, and a most important division is that between the living and the non-living. The bulk of Aristotle's natural works deal with the life-world. It is soul that distinguishes the living from the non-living thing. Are we surprised that any living thing is taken to have a soul? Not if we see that "soul" means the principle of vital activities. Under the influence of our religious tradition, we tend to equate soul with human soul. "What does it profit a man if he gain the whole world and suffer the loss of his own soul?" Rabbits and snails and dandelions do not face such awesome alternatives. Of course we all know people whose pets are regarded by them as peers, persons in disguise, communicating in subtle ways with their owners. The application of "soul" to all living things by Thomas is not based on such sentimentality. Of course, he will be insisting on the dramatic differences between the levels of life and the uniqueness of the human soul. It alone of corporeal forms survives death.

Thomas Aquinas's commentary on Aristotle's *On the Soul* was begun in 1268 in Rome and completed in Paris later that same year. It is the first of some dozen commentaries Thomas would compose at a particularly busy and stressful time of his life. Teaching, disputing, preaching, writing other major works, Thomas somehow found time to write expositions of Aristotle which, if we had nothing else of Thomas's, would suffice to earn him a prominent place in the ranks of philosophers of the West. Young as he was, this was late afternoon in Thomas's life. He would be dead in 1274, not yet 50. It would of course be wrong to imagine that Thomas's interest in the Aristotelian text was a late-blooming passion. Far from it. From his earliest works, he shows an astonishing familiarity with and understanding of Aristotle. It would be difficult to find any writing of his which does not exhibit his assimilation of Aristotle. He made Aristotle his own because he thought Aristotle was for everyone, not a kind of philosophy, but simply Philosophy, just as Aristotle himself was not a philosopher, but the Philosopher. Few texts exhibit the care with which Thomas read Aristotle better than his exposition of the definitions of soul with which Book Two of *On the Soul* begins.

To ask what soul is on the assumption that soul is the distinguishing mark of the living presupposes that we know that there are living as well as non-living things. How do we know this? Is it simply a matter of external observation, the upshot of observing poodles on the one hand and pebbles on the other? We could list any number of things a poodle does that no pebble could do, even though there are many things equally true of them both. We can weigh them, for example, and we don't need one scale for the living and another for the non-living. What seems to characterize the living is that they initiate their own activities and relate to their surroundings in special ways. Is that how interest in the life-sciences begins, by such observations?

As Charles DeKoninck has pointed out in *Introduction à l'étude de l'âme*, our experience of life is an amalgam of external observation and inner experience. It is not simply that I can initiate bodily movements, wave my hand, for example; at the same time I am conscious of the fact that I am bringing this about. My certainty that there is life, that I am alive, is not open to doubt. If we ignored this we would be unable to understand the personal pronoun in the definition of soul. The second definition.

The first definition of soul is this: *the first act of natural organic body*. The soul is the substantial form of the living thing. It is not an incidental form, an accident, as if to be alive were like being in Denver. People escape Denver, but if they die they are no longer the substance that they were. Being alive is an essential characteristic of living things. The road to this definition is paved with a series of distinctions. In order to classify or define we have to find categories in which to put the thing and then indicate how it differs from other things in the same category. Aristotle proposes two series, one for soul, the other for body.

The procedure here is surprising. It is as if we began natural philosophy by asking "What is substantial form?" But that was not the question. The question was, "What is a physical object?" Why do we begin by asking what the soul is rather than what a living body is?

If we remember Plato, we might think Aristotle's procedure is simply a matter of influence. Plato spoke of the soul as something that came and went, its career only fleetingly connected with a body. He compared the two by saying that the body was the ship, the soul the pilot. Aristotle talks something like that in his early dialogs. There is little doubt that from the outset Aristotle is aiming at learning if the human soul can exist by itself. The condition for claiming this would be to find some vital activity which did not essentially involve body. "A further problem presented by the affections of soul is this: are they all affections of the complex of body and soul, or is there any one among them peculiar to the soul itself?" (403a3ff.). It doesn't seem so – anger, courage, desire, and sensation generally are inconceivable without taking into account bodily changes. Oh, one might define anger as "the desire for revenge," but Aristotle dismisses this, saying it is dialectical and does not match what it purports to define. Anger involves bodily tumult as well as a desire for revenge, and both must enter into its definition. But aren't all vital activities like that? If so, the fate of soul and body at death is the same.

Aristotle likens the relation of soul to body to that of the mark of the seal in the wax. How could one possibly separate the impression from the wax? It is made to seem impossible.

The definition of soul as the substantial form of an organic body is taken to be the conclusion of a demonstration. It is derived from the second definition of soul offered:

That which is the first principle of living is the act and form of living bodies.
But the soul is the first principle of living in those things which live.
Therefore, it is the act and form of living body.

As Thomas notes, this is an *a posteriori* demonstration, that is, what is first in our knowledge is not first in reality. "It is because the soul is the form of the living body that it is the principle of the acts of life." It is the recognition of soul as that whereby *we* first move, sense, fear, hope, desire, see, hear, imagine, think, that is the basis for establishing that soul is the substantial form of the living body. Note the personal pronoun. Our experience of ourselves occupies a privileged place in the approach to the life-world. Man emerges as a microcosm in whom modes of life found separately in other things are all present. All things living and non-living share the characteristics of physical things. The simplest mode of life is vegetative, taking nourishment, reproducing. The next level of life subsumes these and adds others, notably sense perception. This is animal life, the animal being a living being endowed with senses. In man all this is subsumed under the distinctive capacity of mind. Man thus looks like an epitome of the cosmos.

But man functions as a whole as the study of living things begins: he is not viewed as the product of adding up various modes of life. Rather these are discerned on the basis of his experience of himself. The recognition that animals exhibit activities like some of ours, and plants too, leads to the recognition of levels of life. They are not the starting points. What we have seen of the general procedure in natural philosophy prepares us for this. The controlling example, the grounding certitude, is our own vital activities.

The soul is the substantial form of the living body. This account draws on what has already been established in the more general analysis of things that come to be as the result of a change. When a substance as such comes to be, prime matter is actuated by a form that makes the result what it is. When Fifi becomes sunburnt in Sarasota, the change is incidental not substantial. Celebrating her birthday, she and her unruly friends are harking back to a change of a more dramatic kind, when Fifi came to be *tout court*. The result of any substantial change is a complex of prime matter and substantial form. The analysis of soul is in effect the analysis of the kind of substantial form that distinguishes living from non-living things.

Things are said to be alive insofar as they manifest vital activities – they move themselves around, they take nourishment and grow, they see and hear and make odd sounds, some imagine and think and speak. Since the living thing is not engaged in any instance of such activities all the time, or in all of them simultaneously, when the living thing does see, for example, it is actually doing what it can do. It has that capacity or faculty. In the vast majority of living things, more than one such capacity exists. If the capacities are noticed on the basis of activities, the question arises as to the relationship between the soul and its capacities. The argument for a distinction between the soul and its capacities is a simple one. If the soul were identical with the ability to see and identical with the ability to hear, actually seeing would be identical with actually hearing. But this flies in the face of our awareness that hearing bears on sounds and seeing on colors. Such reflections lead to the distinction of soul, capacities or faculties, and vital activities.

25

Sense Perception

Just as the definition of soul relies on and hooks up with previous analyses, terms like "form" and "substantial form" being put to new and connected uses, so too when vital activities are analyzed there is a dependence on the analysis of physical objects as such. A new characteristic of a thing is acquired when the subject which lacks but has the capacity for that characteristic comes actually to have it. Sense perception is analyzed on this model. What is going on when we come to see something? This is a change and thus can be analyzed on an analogy with physical changes.

If the soul is the ultimate explanation of our capacity to engage in vital activities, their diversity makes it clear that we must distinguish different powers or capacities of the soul. Seeing and tasting differ, so the capacity to do the one cannot be identical with the capacity to do the other. For this reason, the soul is said to have such capacities and is not identical with them. This is the source of talk of our sense powers and of faculties of the soul. So how should we think of the actuation of such a capacity? How can we understand the passage from not seeing red to seeing red?

The capacity to see is essentially linked to the organ of sight, the eye. The whole body is the organ of the sense of touch and is physically acted on by the things it feels. The physical change is a necessary condition for feeling but is not identical to it. Otherwise we should have to say the eight ball feels the cue ball, the pavement feels my feet, and the hammer and nail inflict terrible pain on one another. (Roald Dahl has a story in which a man hears the grass cry out when it is cut.) So too the eye feels, but not as the organ of sight. The actuation of the capacity to see involves a physical change in the eye; it is acted on by the red object, but seeing is what the eye does, not what is done to it, however essential the latter is. The analogy that suggests itself is that the power of sight is the matter and the color it sees is form. Seeing red is sight's being informed by red. This is not a matter of getting bloodshot eyes. It is not like a physical object's acquiring the quality red, being painted, for example, or ripening in the sun. Having the form of red in seeing is different from the physical object's acquiring a new quality. Thus the analogy is helpful but it has its limitations.

Perceiving understood as a having of the form depends on our prior analysis of physical change. The similarities are there. The difference is crucial. When the physical object acquires the quality red, another numerical instance of that quality comes into being. My seeing red does not involve another numerical instance of the quality. It is here that something most important happens. Seeing red has been analyzed on an analogy with the acquisition of a quality by a physical subject or matter. In order to underscore the different way in which the form red is acquired in seeing, one contrasts it with the reception of form in matter. It is not like that. This is the source of talk of the immateriality of perception. Immaterial here emphasizes that as seen form does not result in another numerical instance of the quality. When this is spoken of as the immaterial reception of a form we must see such talk as dependent on what is being negated. However initially like a physical change coming to see red seemed, we end by stressing the difference.

26

The Immortality of the Human Soul

The notion of immateriality is introduced in speaking of sensation, but it takes on a new and stronger meaning when applied to intellectual activity. The mode of intellectual knowledge, already referred to, bears on the essence, nature, or quiddity abstracted from the incidental properties which attach to it in material individuals.

Is the human soul such that it can subsist or exist independently of the body?

> I reply that it must be said that the principle of intellectual activity, the soul of man, is an incorporeal and subsistent principle. For it is manifest that man can, thanks to intellect, know the natures of all things. But it is necessary that what knows things can have nothing of them in its nature, because that which is naturally in it would impede knowledge of other things, as we see the tongue of one ill affected with choler and bitter humor cannot perceive the sweet but all things seem bitter to him. Therefore if the intellectual principle contained the nature of some body in it it would not be able to know all bodies. But all bodies have a determinate nature. Therefore it is impossible that the intellectual principle be a body.
>
> Similarly, it is impossible that it understands by means of a bodily organ, because the determinate nature of that organ would prevent knowledge of all bodies, just as if there were a determinate color in the pupil and in the vas vitreous, it would see the color of the liquid infused.
>
> Therefore the intellectual principle, which is called mind or intellect, has an activity of its own in which the body is not involved. Only that which subsists on its own can act on its own. (*ST*, Ia, q. 75, a. 2)

That, in a nutshell, is the argument. The text is taken from the *Summa Theologiae* and, in the manner of that work, philosophical conclusions that have been reached in a complicated way are reduced to their essentials, as a reminder to the reader who is taken to be well versed in those philosophical arguments. The range of the senses is wide but each has its own sphere or proper object: the eye can see all colors, therefore it cannot itself be colored. But seeing essentially involves the organ of sight. The range of intellect is unrestricted – *anima est quodammodo omnia* – it can know all bodies and therefore does not itself have a bodily nature. *Intus apparens prohibet extranea.*

To be fully persuasive the proof would have to be as detailed as we find it in *On the Soul*. The upshot is that the human soul has an activity, intellection, which is immaterial. A soul that has this capacity is itself immaterial, with the consequences the text above draws out.

Averroes and Avicenna read Aristotle differently than Thomas does. In different ways they held that Aristotle had proved, not that this and that individual human soul is immaterial, incorporeal, and incorruptible, but that although human thinking involves such a principle, it is not a faculty of the individual soul. Something immaterial can be shown to exist on the basis of the analysis of intellection, but it is not your soul or mine. To this day, the Averroistic position is favored by Aristotelian scholars. They are wrong, as Averroes was wrong. This has been shown to a fare thee well in a little work of Thomas's called *On the Uniqueness of Intellect*. The title refers to the Averroistic position. In this work Thomas shows that the text of Aristotle will not support the Averroistic position and does support the interpretation that he offers.

27

The Opening to Metaphysics

We saw earlier that the final argument of Aristotle's *Physics* had established that there must be a first unmoved mover and that to know this is to know that to be and to be material are not identical. The unmoved mover will be called a separate substance, that is, separate from matter, existing without matter. So too with the recognition that the defining activity of the human soul, intellection, establishes that the human soul is capable of existence apart from the body. Here we have another proven basis for holding that to be and to be material and corporeal are not identical. That there is a science of natural things is clear. That there is mathematics is clear, a science different from natural science. But these two sciences can now be seen to concern themselves with a limited range of being – with corporeal being, with quantified being. If being is not restricted to those modes, the possibility of a third theoretical science suggests itself, the wisdom to which the opening discussion of the *Metaphysics* pointed. And what would be its subject matter? Being as being. That is, not being of this type or that, corporeal or quantified, but being as such. The search for that science represents one of the most profound and rewarding of philosophical tasks.

"There is a science of being as being and of that which belongs to it per se." Thus opens the fourth book of the *Metaphysics*. There is a science beyond natural science and mathematics; like them, it has a subject matter of which it seeks to know the properties. It all seems straightforward. The reader thinks of the scientific methodology developed in the *Posterior Analytics* and imagines it maps on to this enterprise in a more or less ready fashion. But how do you develop a science of everything, of each and any thing insofar as it exists, insofar as it is a being? And why should one wish to ascend into such a stratosphere of abstraction?

Thomas directs our attention to the basis for distinguishing the subject matters of these three theoretical sciences. Theoretical science, as we have seen, bears on things which are not subject to our making or doing. Practical science bears on what can be called "operables," "do-ables," or "make-ables" and by contrast we can call the object of the theoretical the "speculable." Now if there are going to be different theoretical sciences, there must be formal differences in the speculables with which they are concerned. What is essential to the speculable, Thomas asks, since if we can find variations in those essential notes of it, we will have the basis for distinguishing formally different theoretical sciences.

Thomas suggests that there are two essential notes of the speculable, one that derives from the manner of our knowing, the other from the demands of demonstrative syllogism. Intellection grasps the material in an immaterial way. In knowing, there is identity of knower and known, and in the case of intellectual knowledge this entails an immaterial mode on the part of the object. So, removal, separation, from matter is required of the speculable because of the nature of human intellection. Second, it must be necessary. We saw how the demonstrative syllogism which is constitutive of science arrives at necessary truth. The necessary is that which cannot be otherwise. The object of speculation must be immune to change or motion.

Against this background, Thomas concludes: the speculable as speculable is removed from matter and motion. And since the potentiality of matter is the source of motion, we can concentrate on immateriality. The suggestion then is this: insofar as there are formally different ways in which objects are separated from matter there will be formally different theoretical sciences.

> There are some speculables which depend on matter in order to exist since they can only exist in matter, but there is a distinction to be made among them, for (1) some depend on matter both to be and to be understood, for example, things in whose definitions sensible matter is included, which cannot be understood save with sensible matter; e.g. in the definition of man flesh and bones are included. Physics or natural science is concerned with these. (2) But some things, although they depend on matter in order to exist can be understood without it and sensible matter does not enter into their definitions, things like the line and number, with which mathematics is concerned. (3) And there are things which do not depend on matter in order to exist but exist apart from it, whether (a) they never exist in matter, like God and the angels, or (b) are sometimes found in matter and sometimes not, like substance, quality, being, potency, act, one and many, and the like. It may be called theology, that is, divine science (since its chief aim is knowledge of God), or it is sometimes called, metaphysics, that is, beyond the physical, since it is something we learn only after natural science, for we must move from sensible things to things beyond them. It is also called first philosophy insofar as all other sciences take their starting points from it. (*In de Trinitate Boethii*, q. 5, a. 1)

The distinction of the theoretical sciences is thus grounded on formally different modes of defining. Definition is key because the middle term of the demonstrative syllogism constitutive of science is the definition of the subject. We see that mathematics is regarded as a way of knowing physical objects, not as physical, but in terms of abstractable characteristics like line, plane, and so forth. Philosophers have always argued about this, but Thomas holds that there is no special realm of things outside the mind answering to mathematical definitions. Their source is in physical objects and, if they are said to exist, it can only be as edges and surfaces of physical bodies. Euclid alone has looked on beauty bare, but the bareness was in the eye of the beholder: immunity from matter is due to our abstracting mind.

Of course Thomas has to find a basis for this possibility in physical objects. The basis is the sort of layered way in which the categories other than substance are taken to inhere in it. Quantity is the first of the accidents, since all the others presuppose it: e.g., colors require surfaces. Thus, in thought, we can think away the later accidents, and end up with quantified substance, a pure unit. Of course the reverse is not true; we could not think of or define color without reference to quantity. So there is an ontological basis in physical objects for the thinking that characterizes mathematics. But the essential point is this: the fact that the mathematician deals with objects apart from sensible matter does not commit him to the view that these objects exist in the way in which he considers them. This provides us with a first and essential difference between mathematics and metaphysics.

This distinction of the speculative sciences is sometimes spoken of as involving three degrees of abstraction. Thomas suggests another way as well. He assigns a narrower sense to abstraction such that *A* is said to be abstracted from *AB* when it cannot exist apart from *AB*. Then both natural science and mathematics can be called abstract in this narrower and more precise sense. The *way* in which sensible objects are considered and defined in natural sciences is not the *way* in which they exist. What is thought of, the essence, is identical with what exists, but essence as known abstracts from the individual sensible characteristics without which the singular thing could not exist. But the definitions apply to the singulars as the universal does to an instance. In this mathematics differs from natural science.

Mathematics is obviously abstract in this narrower sense. Lines and circles and planes do not exist as they are considered and, if they exist, must do so in physical objects. When abstraction is understood in this narrow sense, we need another word for what goes on in metaphysics. Thomas suggests "separatio." Metaphysics not only considers things without including matter or motion in its accounts, but the things with which it deals, sometimes or always, exist apart from, separately from, matter and motion. Metaphysics bears on immaterial existents. And that leads to a big problem with the characterization of its subject matter in terms of being as being, that is, everything insofar as it is.

28

The Big Problem

One of the recurring difficulties in understanding what is said about metaphysics is to determine whether it deals with a special set of objects – things which exist separately from matter – or with everything whatsoever, insofar as it is. Is it a theology in the sense of dealing with a particular kind of being and thus a special science among others: natural science dealing with material objects, while metaphysics deals with immaterial objects? This question defined Aristotelian studies during much of the twentieth century, under the influence of Werner Jaeger. But it is based on a false dichotomy. The way in which theology was thought of as a special science is a methodological impossibility for Aristotle and Thomas. The only way separate substances can enter into a science of ours is as causes of a subject matter, not as the subject matter itself. That is, the only way there can be a special science of theology is by it being the general science of being as being.

Now on the face of it, and indeed in Aristotelian and Thomistic terms, the commendation of a science as sweeping as metaphysics, one whose subject is everything whatsoever insofar as it is, is paradoxical. We are speaking of the culminating and indeed defining inquiry of philosophy. Metaphysics is a science ranked higher than all others. But what can it mean to commend a science which speaks of the elm tree as being? Is it not a more profound knowledge of the elm tree to know it as a plant, or as a substance? That is vaguer knowledge, not more profound knowledge. But isn't that a fortiori the case when we are told that a thing will be considered, not as a physical object, but as a being? Surely it is better to know that something is a bee than to know simply that it is a being.

Furthermore, when we consider that philosophy is the many-storied effort to arrive at such knowledge as we can of the divine – the point made in the opening chapters of the *Metaphysics* – it seems clear that the culminating science should be described as dealing with separated or immaterial being and not with being as being. Why else did Thomas distinguish separation from abstraction?

> So the intellect is found to distinguish in three ways: one which is founded on the activity of composing and dividing which is properly separation and belongs to divine science or metaphysics; a second founded on the activity whereby the quiddities of things are grasped, the abstraction of form from sensible matter, and this belongs to mathematics; a third based on the same activity where the universal is abstracted from the particular, and this belongs to natural science but is common to all the sciences insofar as every science bears on what is essential and eschews the incidental. (*In de Trin.*, q. 5, a. 3)

That final sentence tells us that metaphysics is characterized by separation but like any science abstracts from what is not essential to its subject matter. Aristotle was thought to have waffled between the view that metaphysics is a general science and that it is a special science, and was unable to resolve the problem, and this text of Thomas might invite the same kind of interpretation. I have said this problem is based on a false dichotomy. In the next chapter, let us look at the difficult matters that underwrite that judgment.

29

The Two Theologies Revisited

Earlier we had occasion, in our discussion of the way in which Thomas distinguishes philosophy from theology, to speak of two theologies, that with which philosophy ends, its culminating effort, and that which is based on revelation, Sacred Scripture. As it happens, in the commentary on Boethius's *De Trinitate*, that we have been consulting for Thomas's views on the distinction of speculative science into three kinds, there is a discussion of the way in which God enters into philosophy, on the one hand, and into scriptural theology on the other. It occurs in the article that puts the question: "Does divine science deal with things separate from matter and motion?" What could be said against a negative answer to that question? Thomas put forth eight objections, some of which are more relevant to our present interest than others. The first argues that God can only be known by way of his visible effects, which are material and mobile. (Of course he refers to Romans 1:19–20.)

The fifth objection is this: "the divine science which occupies the third stage of speculative philosophy is the same as metaphysics, whose subject is being and especially the being that is substance, as is clear from *Metaphysics IV*." But being and substance do not abstract from matter, otherwise there wouldn't be any material being. So it cannot be that divine science is one that abstracts from matter.

The sixth objection reminds us of the methodology of any science. A science considers not only its subject matter, but the parts and properties of its subject. But it is said that being is the subject of divine science, so it should be concerned with all beings, and surely matter and motion are instances of being and should therefore pertain to the consideration of the metaphysician whose science cannot be said to abstract from them.

Thomas next counters with arguments in support of a negative answer to the question posed. To begin with, Aristotle in *Metaphysics VI* (1026a16) says that first philosophy is concerned with the separable – that is, separable from matter – and immobile. But first philosophy is divine science. Ergo, etc.

And shouldn't the most noble of sciences be concerned with the noblest? But surely immaterial and immobile things are the noblest. Moreover, Aristotle at the outset of the *Metaphysics* tells us that divine science is concerned with the first principles and causes (981b28 ff.). But these are immaterial and immobile. And it is with such things that divine science is concerned.

When Werner Jaeger came upon this problem early in the twentieth century it was these same texts of Aristotle that worried him. It was his judgment that Aristotle had been unable to solve the problem, and indeed that the elements of the problem represented different geological layers in the development of Aristotle. When the emphasis was on the divine, separate and elsewhere, we are close to Aristotle's long sojourn in the Platonic Academy; when the emphasis is on the characteristics common to all the things around us we are closer to the mature empirical Aristotle. This delivered Aristotle over to the philologists who vied with one another to come up with imaginative and scarcely credible accounts of the formation of the Aristotelian corpus. But what if there is no problem? Or, rather, what if the problem admits of a solution? Thomas's approach to it is a model for the student of Aristotle.

We invoke the notion of science in the phrase "divine science." Every science studies its subject matter by considering the principles of the subject, science being obtained when one achieves knowledge of principles, as Aristotle reminded us at the beginning of the *Physics* (184a10–12). But there are two kinds of principle:

> Some are in themselves complete natures yet are principles of other things as well, as the heavenly bodies are principles of earthly bodies, and simple bodies of the mixed. Such things are scientifically considered not only as principles but as things themselves. Thus they are considered, not only in the science concerned with the things they cause but they have a distinct science of their own. For example, there is a distinct natural science devoted to heavenly bodies apart from that in which they play an explanatory role in lower bodies. So too there is a science of the elements in which they are studied in themselves and not as principles of mixed bodies.
>
> Other principles are not complete things in themselves but only principles of nature, as unity of number and point of line, and matter and form of physical bodies. Such principles are treated only in the science which treats the things of which they are the principles. (*In de Trin.*, q. 5, a. 4, c.)

Thomas goes on to observe that principles are common to a given subject matter and so there must be principles common to all beings insofar as they are beings. But principles are common in two different ways. Some principles are predicably common; that is, they can be said of everything covered by the subject matter. "Form is common to all forms," in the sense that it is predicated of them all; they are all called forms. As opposed to what? Well, some things are causally common to many effects; that is, something numerically one is the cause of all generable things. We understand the contrast. In universal predication, the one thing that is said of the many is not something numerically one, as if all men were the same man. However, a universal cause is not an abstract idea, but a single thing whose causality extends to many. What is the importance of this distinction for the question before us?

There are common principles of all beings not only in the first way, a way the philosopher calls in *Metaphysics XII* (1070a31 ff.) "according to analogy," but also in the second way such that there are numerically distinct things which are the causes of things, the principles of accidents being reduced to the principles of substance, and the principles of corruptible substances to those of incorruptible substances, and so in a hierarchical order they are reduced to that which is the principle of the being of all beings. That is, to God.

The application of these distinctions is as follows. Although he has illustrated the two ways in which principles can be common by appeal to a plurality of natural sciences, say, astronomy, as opposed to the way in which the sun and moon are invoked to explain changes on earth, he does not take Aristotle to hold that there are two philosophical sciences, ontology and theology, the latter of which would have God as its subject matter. There is no way we can come to philosophical knowledge of the divine except through his effects. First causes may be most perfect in themselves and in that sense most knowable, there being more in them to be known, but with respect to them our intellect is as the eye of the nightbird in sunlight (Thomas refers to *Metaphysics II* (993b9–11)), and we can attain knowledge of them only insofar as we are led to knowledge of the causes from effects – and here he refers to Romans 1:20.

> Hence it is that divine things are treated by philosophers only insofar as they are the principles of all things, and thus are pursued in that discipline which studies what is common to all beings the subject of which is being and being, which is why they call it divine science. (Ibid.)

That is it, so far as our natural powers of knowing are concerned, so far as philosophy is concerned. But the foregoing distinctions were not made in vain. "There is another way of knowing such things, not as made manifest through their effects, but as they make themselves manifest." If God should reveal himself to men, telling them things about himself that could not be known through his effects, there becomes possible a theology or divine science in a sense quite different from that of the philosophers. But that revelation has been made, in Sacred Scripture and in the Incarnate Word, such that there is a set of truths about God which are accepted, not on the basis of understanding but on the basis of faith.

> So there are two kinds of theology or divine science, one in which divine things are considered not as the subject of the science but as causes of the subject, and such is the theology the philosophers pursue, which is also called metaphysics; and another in which these divine things are considered in themselves as the subject of the science, and this is the theology given in Sacred Scripture. Both are concerned with things which exist separately from matter and motion, but differently, insofar as things can be said to be separated from matter in two ways,

first, when the nature of the separated things is such that it could never be found in matter and motion, as God and the angels are said to be separate from matter; second, when they are such that it is not of their nature that they be found in matter and motion; they can be without matter and motion, but are sometimes found in matter and motion, such as being and substance and potency and act are separate from matter and motion. They do not depend on matter and motion since they can exist apart from them and in this they differ from mathematicals which never exist except in matter even though they can be understood without sensible matter. Philosophical theology treats of things separate in this second way as its subject matter and of things separate in the first way as causes of its subject. The theology of Sacred Scripture treats things separate in the first way as its subject matter though it also considers material and mobile things when this is required to manifest the divine. (Ibid.)

Early in his career, in his early thirties, Thomas was thus able to distinguish with remarkable clarity the two theologies, that of the philosopher and that derived from Sacred Scripture. But however clear the distinction, it raises a host of questions. What does it mean to say that being and substance and so forth are sometimes material and sometimes not? How are we supposed to know this? Does what God reveals of himself bypass our natural mode of knowing with its dependence on the senses and, if not, is the distinction offered here jeopardized? Scripture is of course written down, to be read, and St Paul says faith comes through hearing – *fides ex auditu* – suggesting that revelation too involves a passage from effects to cause. But our immediate concern must be to grasp Thomas's understanding of the way in which theology is lodged in metaphysics, the divine functioning as a causal explanation of all the things that are, of being as being.

30

Being as Being

Metaphysics is said to study being as being, that is, whatever is just insofar as it is a being. This may seem to suggest that there is some identical mark or note which can be found in anything that is, but a moment's reflection makes clear that, in the Aristotelian phrase, "being is said in many ways." There is no single meaning of the term under which we can gather all the things that are, indeed things are not things in the same sense of the term. There is a medieval image of the fleetingness of life: a bird flies in a hall at one end and exits at the other. But however brief its existence, the bird and its color and movement do not exist in the same way; they are not beings in a uni-vocal sense. But isn't that what the claim to study all beings *as beings* suggests? And yet, if there is no single sense of the term, a single science of all beings seems chimerical.

Of course, this is a problem Aristotle puts to himself as he sets out to establish a science beyond natural science and mathematics. He begins with the confident assertion that there is a science of being as being, speaks of it as the subject matter of the science, and notes that in any science we study not only what the subject matter is but the properties that belong to it, and so too it must be in metaphysics. But one of the conditions of scientific demonstration is that terms be used in the same sense and, in the concatenation of proofs that make up a science in the sense of a body of knowledge, the things first and generally known must be applicable in the same sense to things studied later in their specificity. The analysis of physical objects with which natural philosophy begins is the most general treatment of such things, but it must be true of all the things subsequently studied however they differ from one another in other ways. There are truths common to living and non-living things insofar as they are physical objects. Are there truths common to all the things that are in the same way? This would require a single meaning of "being" and what would that be?

In order to pursue this as Aristotle and Thomas do, we must invoke a number of distinctions they make in the way in which terms are common or shared by a number of things, things of which they are predicated. These are not sophisticated distinctions, but like so much of the explanatory apparatus we have thus far encountered, plucked from ordinary thought and usage. Aristotle begins the *Categories* with these distinctions, so to speak, on the first page of his works.

When we hear it said that a carpenter hit his nail when he was nailing boards, and that is why he is dancing around in the yard uttering profanities, we have no difficulty in understanding. When Cinderella goes to the ball where she dances on the balls of her feet and the next day goes to a ball game we are not puzzled by the report of her activities. Nor when the peculating scientist is found studying cells in his cell. English being our native tongue, we handle such uses of "nail" and "ball" and "cell" and untold others without being misled. Indeed, they seldom arrest our attention as they are made to do in puns and poetry. "Will they bill and coo when the bills come due?" "What matters if my love be fair if she is not fair to me?" If this is ambiguity it does not mislead. And it is ambiguity.

When such uses are thought about we may of course be tempted by the thought that "nail" has the same meaning in the two uses given, that "ball" has a single meaning whether we are talking of a dance, a part of the foot, or what was just hit out of the park for a home run. Nor might cell phones deter us from thinking that "cell" means the same thing however it is used. This is not a temptation we should overcome by submitting to it in a Wildean fashion. It is fairly inescapable that "nail" just happens to be used in oddly different ways – in Shakespeare it is a musical instrument. The fact that this diversity of meaning does not mislead us is not an argument for a single meaning.

What is common to them all, however, is that we find a plurality of things which share a common term which has quite different meanings as predicated of each of them. How can it be the same term if there is no single meaning underwriting the sameness? Well, it is spelled the same way, it is the same orthographic symbol, and it sounds the same. Sounding the same does not always give a term of the same spelling, however, so that there are more linguistic jokes which depend on the spoken than the written language. "It was a good buy" the improvident wife explains and her exasperated spouse puts on his hat and says "Goodbye indeed." Things which share a common term that has a plurality of unrelated meanings are said to be named equivocally.

As opposed to what? Things are said to be named univocally when they share a common name that has the same meaning as predicated of each of them. Those painted appendages at the ends of her fingers are all called "nail" in the same sense; the ball of Cinderella's left foot is called such in the same sense as that of her right foot; the cell next to the imprisoned biologist is a cell in the same sense as his. It is to be noticed that equivocity and univocity can be illustrated with the same terms.

If these were the only possibilities to account for the way in which "being" is said of all the things that are, metaphysics would be impossible. The third account of shared terms appealed to in discussing the subject of metaphysics should not be thought of as fashioned ad hoc to handle a difficulty. This third kind of common or shared term, what Thomas called the analogical term, permeates the thought of Thomas as it did Aristotle's. Indeed, we have been insisting on it from the very beginning of our account of Thomas's philosophy. "Form" is a term with multiple meanings, as is "potency," "matter," and just about every key term in Thomas's philosophical vocabulary. Terms which in some uses are univocal in others are analogical. What precisely is meant by an analogous term?

31

Analogy

If terms are used equivocally when they are predicated of several things in such a way that they have a different meaning in each instance, if terms are univocal when they are predicated of several things and bear exactly the same meaning in each instance, the analogous term may be thought of as midway between them. The example Aristotle and Thomas most often give – ad nauseam, one is tempted to say – is "healthy." Your parakeet is healthy, the seed you feed it is healthy, and his brilliant plumage is healthy. If we should take this to exemplify equivocity we would be made uneasy by the difference of this example from that of "ball" et al. We would despair of finding a reason why the same word bears the different meanings it does in the uses enumerated. It just happens to have them all; there is no link among them. But that does not seem to cover the example of "healthy." We sense that there is such a link here, yet it falls short of the univocal use of a term. We would be hard put to come up with a meaning for healthy that is unvaried in the three uses given. When the parakeet is said to be healthy reference is made to its physical condition. For Thomas, as for Shakespeare, health consists in a balance of the four humors; our explanation would be different. But the account of healthy as said of your parakeet would not be exactly the same as when it is said of birdseed and plumage. But surely there is a link.

When the bird is said to be healthy it is the subject of health whether defined in the medieval manner or in the modern. Birdseed is called healthy because it causes or preserves that condition in the parakeet. Plumage is called healthy because it is a sign of the bird's health. Dull or molting feathers would alarm you and you would be on the phone to the bird doctor. It is helpful to think of this variety in terms of a schema:

Healthy = _____ health.

There are different ways of filling in the blank to attain a meaning or account: "subject of;" "cause of;" "sign of." There is a link between these meanings. Is it health? Health is a component of the meaning of "healthy," not its meaning as such. Your parakeet isn't health. One of the meanings, one result of filling in the blank, is paramount and regulative of the others. Which one? Healthy as meaning "subject of health" is either what is meant or it is a component of what is meant. Birdseed is the cause of health in the bird that is the subject of health; brilliant plumage is a sign of health in the bird that is the subject of health. We grasp some meanings by referring to one of them. The first or regulative meaning of a term used in this way is called the primary analogate. Whether there is only one or several such secondary meanings, the primary analogate must be understood in understanding it or them.

This kind of community is midway between pure equivocation and simple univocity. In things said analogously there is not one account, as in univocals, nor totally diverse accounts, as in equivocals, but the term that is thus said in many ways signifies diverse proportions to some one thing, as 'healthy' said of urine signifies the sign of the health of the animal and said of medicine it signifies the cause of the same health. (*ST*, Ia, q.13, a. 5)

Thomas uses the following second-order or logical vocabulary to express this. "Health" is the thing signified, the *res signficata*, and "subject of," "cause of," and "sign of" are ways of signifying it, *modi significandi*. The *res* and *modus* are components of the accounts or *rationes* in play when the term is used. This terminology enables Thomas to give a crisp comparison of the three kinds of common term.

> The equivocal, analogous and univocal are distinguished differently from one another. The equivocal is divided according to the things signified (*res significatae*), the univocal is divided according to diverse differences, but the analogous is divided according to diverse modes. (*I Sent.*, d. 22, q. 1, a. 3, ad 2)

There is nothing arcane or technical about these observations. Nor is analogous usage rare or as such metaphysical. It pervades natural philosophy, as we have indicated. But it is indeed the means to solving the puzzles that arise in trying to understand "being as being" as the subject matter of a science beyond natural philosophy and mathematics.

32

Being as Analogous

Since being has many meanings, the question must arise as to how there can be a science, rather than sciences, of being. Among the questions Aristotle had developed in Book Three of the *Metaphysics*, the book of problems or aporias that must be solved if the science we are seeking is to be found, was whether or not this science considered substance alone or accidents as well. That encapsulates the great problem confronting such a science. Where is the solution to be found?

With respect to the first, he uses this argument. When things share a common predicate, although it is not univocally but analogously predicated of them, they can be considered in the same science. But being is said in this way of all beings. Therefore all beings fall to the consideration of one science, which considers being as being, that is, both substance and accident. (*Metaphysics IV*, lect. 1, n. 534)

The argument presupposes that "being" is said analogously of substance and accident, and that this supplies sufficient unity for a science. In commenting on the establishment of the first presupposition, Thomas rehearses the threefold distinction of common terms we have discussed. He gives the following account of analogy. "Sometimes however [a term is predicated] according to accounts that are partly diverse and partly not diverse: diverse insofar as they imply different relations, one insofar as they are relations to something one and the same, and this is to be predicated analogically, that is, proportionally, insofar as each refers to that one thing."

It might be noted parenthetically that one will not find the Greek for analogous in the text of Aristotle here. Aristotle speaks of "things said in many ways with reference to one," but the account he gives of that is the account that Thomas gives of analogous terms. Aristotle uses *analogia* and *kat' analogian* frequently, but not in this key text. For all that, the commentary is not offering an explanation different from the text (see my *Aquinas and Analogy*).

Thomas gives this important account of the one which is variously referred to in the many accounts of the common term.

Again, it should be known that the one to which the diverse relations refer in analogous terms is numerically one and not one in account as is the case with things designated univocally. Therefore, although being is said in many ways, it is not said equivocally, but with respect to one, not to something which is only one in account, but which is one as a definite nature. As is clear in the appended examples. (Ibid., n. 536)

The examples are "healthy," and "medical," which both exemplify what is meant by an analogous name, but which differ from "being." In the case of "healthy" the one thing referred to is the end of health, that is, a final cause; in the case of "medical" the one thing referred to is an efficient cause, the art of medicine which is had by the physician and extended to his instruments and prescriptions. The one referred to in the case of the analogous term "being" is rather one subject, not one efficient or final cause.

Some things are called beings or are said to be because they them-selves have existence, that is, substances, which are chiefly and in the first place what the term means. Others are called being because they are passions or properties of the substances, that is, the per se acci-dents of substances. Some things are called being because they are the way to substance, such as generation and movement. Yet others are called being because they are the corruptions of substance, and because corruption terminates in privation as generation in form, fittingly the privations of substantial forms are said to be. Again, qualities or acci-dents are called beings, because they are active or generative of sub-stance or of those things which in one of the ways mentioned are related to substance, or in some other way. So too the negations of things related to substance or indeed of substance itself are said to be, which would not be said if existence did not belong in some way to negation. (Ibid., n. 539)

The numerically one, as opposed to merely conceptually one thing to which all the secondary meanings of "being" refer, is substance. This is why the science of being as being concentrates on substance, which is the source of such unity as it has.

33

Substance

It will of course occur to us that the problems associated with the community of "being" do not go away when the primacy of substance is recognized. "Substance" too is going to have to be recognized as an analogous term since it cannot mean the same thing as predicated of physical objects and of, say, angels. If we say that metaphysics concentrates on substance as such and is indifferent to the distinc-tion between corporeal and incorporeal substances, we would be assuming that it is a univocal term. But surely it is not predicated univocally of men and angels. Only if we recognize this problem will we be in a position to grasp the trajectory of metaphysics, its methodology.

When Thomas in *On Being and Essence* lays out what is meant by essence, he begins with the nature or quiddity of material things. Only after he has clarified this does he proceed to the similar but different meaning essence has in the angels. So too when Aristotle turns to substance in the *Metaphysics* he dwells at great length on material substance. Only in this way can he fashion a meaning of the term which makes it applicable to separated substances. There is no discussion of substance as such, as if it were univocal; there is only a discussion of types of substance, beginning with material substance and proceeding to separated substance, the latter account dependent on the former. That this is the heart and soul of metaphysical procedure is clear from the most misunderstood book in Aristotle's *Metaphysics*, Book Five or Delta.

This book is sometimes referred to, somewhat mysteriously, as a philosophical lexicon. One edition actually puts it first, before the other books, as if were an initiation to Aristotelian jargon having no functional role in the specific work in which it is found. Those who followed Werner Jaeger were unanimous in regarding it as misplaced in this treatise. A glance at Book Five might suggest a random selection of terms. Principle, cause, element, nature, necessary, one and many, being, substance, and so on. What is the point of the book? Thomas casts light on this in a way that distinguishes him from almost every other commentator.

The things considered in this work, he observes, are common to all and they are not said univocally but analogously of them, that is according to priority and posteriority, as was explained in Book Four. Any science considers its subject, the properties of its subject, and the causes of its subject. The apparently random list of terms refers to these three. "First Aristotle determines distinct meanings of names which signify causes, secondly those which signify the subject, thirdly those which signify the properties of being as being" (*Metaphysics V*, lect. 1, n. 749). In each case, a primary meaning is developed as the term applies to physical or material things, and on the basis of this meanings are fashioned which enable the term to be predicated of immaterial things. Book Five is utterly functional within the treatise as a whole and underscores the method of metaphysics.

The first step in the analysis of substance is to argue that it is prior to accident in knowledge, in definition, and in time.

> To be white is not to be simply but in a certain respect. This is evident from the fact that when something becomes white we do not say that

it has come to be simply but that it comes to be white. But when Socrates becomes a man it is said that he has come to be simply. It is clear then that to be a man signifies to be simply whereas to be white signifies to be in a certain respect. (*Metaphysics VII*, lect. 1, n. 1256)

The four senses of "substance" that are taken from received opinion to be analyzed are essence (*quod quid erat esse*), the universal, the genus, and the subject. The last is what is called first substance in the *Categories*, that is, particular things like Socrates, Fido, that tree, and the like.

The meaning of "substance" given here is practically the same as that given in the *Categories*, since by subject here is understood first substance. But what he calls the genus and universal, which pertains to genus and species, are contained under second substance. He adds essence here, something omitted there because it does not fall within the order of the categories save as their principle. It is neither a genus not species nor individual but the formal principle of them all. (Ibid., n. 1275)

As for the subject, or particular, it is divided into form, matter, and the composite of the two. Nothing could be clearer: the analysis of substance begins with material substance. Are there separate substances? "This will be determined below in Book Twelve, but before that can be determined we must first posit and describe what in sensible things is substance, in which substance is manifest, and this he does in Books Seven and Eight" (ibid., lect. 1, n. 1269). But the analysis of sensible substance leads to the recognition that, in the particular material thing, form is more substance than is matter. Form is act, matter is potency, and act is naturally prior to potency (1278). This is a crucial point. If form is more substance than matter, subsistent form will provide a way of speaking of separated substances, and a way of understanding what is meant by saying that they are more substances than are material substances.

In this we see the point of the metaphysical analysis of material substance. In itself it may seem simply to go over ground already established in natural philosophy, but what is sought is an intimation of what separated substance might be. That is the telos of the work, which is why Book Twelve can be seen as its culmination.

34

Presuppositions of Metaphysics

Metaphysics may be described as the development of the description of what immaterial substance is like and of a vocabulary to express these descriptions or accounts. Is this merely an exercise in intellectual imagination? That is what it would be if all that were being done is developing conceptual possibilities, an account of what immaterial substances are should there be any. But, as we have seen, the possibility of a science beyond natural science and mathematics is based on reasoned conviction, on proofs, that there actually are things which exist apart from matter and motion, namely, the Prime Mover and the human soul. That this is the case is stated again and again in the course of Thomas's commentary on the *Metaphysics* If there are no separated substances then natural philosophy would be first philosophy.*

This plain talk is sometimes questioned or downgraded, and thought to have been trumped by the statement in Thomas's "personal" (and youthful) work that substance and act and potency and the like are immaterial because they are sometimes found in matter and sometimes not. But how would we know that some substances are immaterial without a proof?

----

* See the following paragraphs in the commentary: nn. 46, 181, 398, 563, 593, 690, 748, 1170, 2267, 2517.

35

God and Metaphysics

When Thomas gives a capsule version of the proof of an unmoved mover in the *Summa Theologiae* he adds that this is what men mean by God. Metaphysics is undertaken to see what more can be known and said of separated substances, especially of God. And in the *Metaphysics* we find a magnificent description of God: thought thinking itself. Thomas follows closely Aristotle's painstaking elaboration making it inescapable that the control on what can be said of the divine intellect is what we know of our own. It is by way of negating limitations of human intellection that one comes to an understanding of the divine. If "intellect" is said of man and God it must be analogously common to them.

We come now to one of the great paradoxes of Thomas's thought. The conception of philosophy he learned from Aristotle arranged all intellectual disciplines in an order that ascended to knowledge of the divine. The wisdom that we seek will be had when we have attained such knowledge. We have been forewarned that this culminating discipline, however noble its object, will fall short of perfect exemplification of the criteria of demonstrative science. Those criteria are invoked in the development of the science, but even more as they are obstacles in the way of their ready application, for example, establishing how being as being could be a subject of a demonstrative syllogism.

And the whole conception of how the human mind passes painstakingly from ignorance to knowledge, with its dependence on the senses every step of the way, make it problematical that there are immaterial things or, if there are, that we could know it. Many seem blithely to assume that simply the use of such abstract terms as "being" and "substance" opens the gate to metaphysics. But until and unless we know these terms have application to beings that are not material they will simply be a vaguer way of speaking of rocks and trees and centipedes. Only proofs which arise in the course of doing natural philosophy open the door to a science beyond it and mathe-

matics. But that science, from the point of view of scientific methodology, is most peculiar. It seems to spend most of its time going over
familiar ground, rehearsing the analyses of natural philosophy, but
there is method in this. This is a sustained and difficult effort to
fashion a vocabulary that can be applied to immaterial or separated
substances. We want to know more about God and that requires us
to know more about physical objects. Substance, act, intelligence –
these are some of the divine attributes that emerge in the *Metaphysics*. These are the *communia entis*, analogously, not univocally,
common to God and creature.

At the outset of the *Metaphysics* we were reminded that the
human intellect is like the eye of a nightbird in the light of the sun.
Nonetheless, a little knowledge, however imperfect, of the divine is
preferable to a vast amount of knowledge of lesser things. A false
dichotomy, of course, since we can achieve knowledge of the divine
only by riding piggyback on knowledge of sensible things. The enormous achievement of Aristotle in Book Twelve of the *Metaphysics*
obviously elicited the admiration of Thomas Aquinas. If there is any-
where we might expect him to downplay the work of Aristotle it is
when we arrive at these efforts to describe God. But Thomas is
clearly far more impressed with what the human mind unaided can
achieve than its comparison with the rich Christian tradition of
divine attributes. And when he does turn to the latter he is insistent
on the limitations of our knowledge of God, whether or not it is aided
by revelation.

If names are common to God and creature they cannot be
univocally common and, if they were simply equivocal, it would
not much matter what we affirmed or denied of God. Since it does
matter, as is clear from the care with which Aristotle explains
what is meant by pure act and thought thinking itself, we must ask
how such terms can be common to creatures and God, to material
and immaterial things. The same of course is true of the divine
attributes conveyed by Sacred Scripture. In both cases, Thomas
appeals to the notion of analogy to see his way clear. His teaching on
the divine names is the most exalted employment of the notion of
analogous names. But, as with the invocation of analogy to discuss
the subject of metaphysics, we should note that analogy itself is a
commonplace of Aristotle's and Thomas's philosophy. Consequently
we are faced with a new application of a familiar doctrine, as is
clear by the invocation of "healthy" to remind us of what analogous
names are.

Some things said of God, e.g. Lord, creator, are terms that relate him to creatures and others are negations of creaturely limitations, e.g. eternal (timeless), immaterial, and the like. Analogous names are those which state something positive about God, e.g. wise. In analyzing such names, Thomas invokes the second-order vocabulary we mentioned earlier, the *res significata* and the *modus significandi*, as constituents of a *ratio* or meaning. This enables him to employ the threefold approach of "Pseudo-Denis": affirmation; negation; eminence. God is wise; God is not wise; God is wise in a way we cannot know. How are affirmations and denials of the same term possible? When God is said to be wise, it is the *res significata*, the perfection of wisdom, that is thought of; when he is said not to be wise, it is the creaturely *modus significandi* that is thought of. Every name said of God is defective with respect to the mode of signifying: *omne nomen cum defectu est quantum ad modum significandi* (I *Summa contra Gentiles* 30). But such perfections as wisdom do not as such involve a limitation. Furthermore, although it is created wisdom that provides the springboard for the extension of the name, when God is said to be wise we do not simply mean that he is the cause of created wisdom. Wisdom is affirmed of him. The way of eminence underscores the fact that we cannot know how God is wise, but that he is so is not in doubt.

The analogical extension to God of certain terms first applicable to creatures – those whose *res significata* does not involve any imperfection – suggests a plurality in God: wisdom, justice, understanding, etc. Although such perfections do not intrinsically involve imperfection, their multiplicity is a sign of their origin in our knowing of perfections as found in creatures. And this multiplicity is in itself a sign that we cannot understand *what* God is. Thomas insists on this both early and late, and it may seem to suggest that he is saying that we end up in total ignorance of what we are saying when we speak of God. Of course this is not his point; his point is the imperfect and defective way in which we grasp and express the divine perfection. It is not the denial of the *res significata* of, say, wisdom of God. When Thomas says that we cannot know the quiddity of God – or of the angels, for that matter – he has in mind the limitations of the affirmative divine attributes. This limitation is not restricted to philosophical efforts to extend terms first used of creatures to God. It is found as well in those perfections God attributes to himself in Sacred Scripture. The human mode of knowing is still operative in religious faith.

And thus these [immaterial] substances are not sufficiently made known on the basis of similitude (*per viam similitudinis*) nor by way of causality (*per viam causalitatis*), because the things caused by these substances in inferior things are not effects adequate [proprotionate] to their power, which would enable us to come to know what such a cause is [its essence]. Accordingly in this life we cannot know the quiddities of such things either by way of natural knowledge or even by way of revelation, because the light of divine revelation is received by us according to our manner of knowing, as Denis says. Hence although we are raised by revelation to know something which would otherwise remain unknown to us, this is not by some mode of knowing other than that dependent on sensible things. (*In de Trinitate*, q. 6, a. 3)

36

Ipsum esse Subsistens

As if in response to the realization that the very plurality of the divine names is an index of the exiguous knowledge we have of God, Thomas asks if there isn't some name which would overcome this, some name which could be called, as it were, God's proper name. Something found in Exodus suggests that there is such a name. When, in the biblical text, Moses asks God what his name is so he can tell others, God replies, "Tell them that He Who Is has sent me to you." This is high warrant indeed for taking He Who Is to be the proper name of God. But what can it mean?

Thomas discusses this in many places, but the early discussion in his commentary on Boethius's *De Hebdomadibus* is particularly rich and provides an occasion to speak of the distinction between essence and existence. The question of the little treatise is "Whether things are good just insofar as they are," and Boethius proposes to treat it *more geometrico*. That is, he will first set down a number of axioms, truths which are *per se notae*, or self-evident, and employ them to answer the question. The very first axiom is *diversum est esse et id quod est* (what a thing is and that it is differ). It is Thomas's reflection on this axiom that brings him to God's "proper name."

The infinitive to be, *esse*, occurs in finite forms in affirmations such as *S* is *P*, in which both the subject and predicate terms can be taken to restrict the range of existence. If the predicate term is some incidental attribute of the substance it expresses incidental existence, *esse accidentale*. If we simply say that a substance is, we express *esse substantiale*. What kind of predicate is "exists" when we say that Socrates exists? It is the assertion of the actuality of Socrates, that is, of a certain kind of thing, a human being. It would seem that to be is to be something or other, some kind of being, but what a thing is and its actual existence differ in the sense that it is not of the nature of the thing, some constituent of its essence, that it should exist. Were this the case it would necessarily exist simply by dint of being a kind of thing.

This distinction between essence and existence in physical objects is not put forward as some sophisticated metaphysical truth. It is an axiom, that is, self-evident. It stands in need of the kind of clarification Thomas provides, but it does not stand in need of proof. Its denial would land one in the kind of difficulty mentioned: if a thing exists it necessarily exists – if existence were of its essence. But that is manifestly not true of physical objects. For them to exist is for a form actually to inhere in a matter. That actual inherence is not the form nor the matter but an actuality distinct from them.

The analysis Thomas offers in terms of the restriction of the range of to be or *esse* by subject and predicate terms in a proposition enables him to explain Boethius's use of participation. When Socrates exists, he is not existence, but shares in or participates in existence, his existence being measured by his nature or essence. He is a *human* being.

Thomas in his commentary introduces a difficulty Boethius did not dwell on, and that is the status of separated substances in the plural. That sensible things, physical objects, have an essence distinct from their existence is fairly easily grasped. But the way in which Thomas has analyzed it enables him to handle the problem of separated substances. Unlike physical objects, these are not compounds of form and matter. A way of thinking of them as substances is as pure forms, subsistent forms. For a physical object to exist is for its form actually to inhere in its matter. The essence or nature is the measure of its existence: it is a being of a certain kind. It participates in existence up to a point. If there are separated substances understood as subsistent forms, their forms will be what distinguishes them from one another. In physical objects existence comes through the form – *forma dat esse*. Does the initial axiom – *diversum est esse et id quod est* – apply to separated substances or forms? The very fact of their plurality – this one is not that – suggests that we can think of their form as a participation in existence, a kind of existence, accordingly, not existence as such. In their own way, they like physical objects are finite, that is, particpations in existence. Their essences too are distinct from their existence.

Of course much more can be said of this, the control always being what we know of sensible things, but Thomas moves on to the case of utterly simple being, God.

> That alone will be truly simple which does not participate in existence, whose existence does not inhere in it but is rather subsistent. And this can only be one because if existence had nothing in it which is not existence, as has been said, it is impossible that existence is multiplied by some diversifying factor, and because it has nothing else conjoined to it it follows that it will be the subject of no accident. This simple thing, one and sublime, will be God. (*In Boethii de Hebdomadibus*, 2, lines 249–58)

The "proper" name of God, accordingly, is Subsistent Existence, *ipsum esse subsistens*. That will always be Thomas's gloss on the response God gives to Moses, "He Who Is has sent me to you." To say of God that he is wise or just, however true, can sound like saying that he is a kind of being. When it is recognized that he is not a kind of being, but being itself, these attributes may be imagined as coalescing in the *esse* they seem to restrict. In calling God Subsistent Existence, accordingly, he is recognized as the summation of all perfections which are unified in him in a way that quite exceeds our capacity to comprehend.

This does not entail that the divine attributes are synonyms, as if "just" and "merciful" had the same meaning as said of God. Their origin in our knowledge of created perfections is the source of the different accounts we give of them. But the move to Subsistent Existence seeks to overcome the imperfection implied by the plurality of divine attributes. Apart from the analysis we have just sketched this would make little sense to us. And even after the analysis is made we end by recognizing that we do not comprehend how the perfections signified by the different divine attributes are one in God. But we know they must be, on penalty of ascribing to God the imperfections of creatures. Only if his effects exhausted his causal power, so to say, and were proportionate or commensurate with it would they enable us to see what God is. But they do enable us to have some knowledge, however imperfect, of him. If we end in ignorance, in the sense of non-comprehension of what God is, it is a learned ignorance, a *docta ignorantia*.

37

The Moral Order

We recall the four orders Thomas distinguished at the outset of his commentary on the *Nicomachean Ethics*. We have said something of the first two orders. The third is the moral order, to which we now turn.

"There is a third order that reason in deliberating establishes in the operations of the will." The locus of morality is human acts, acts of will directed by reason. Clarity about the human act, accordingly, is clarity about the moral order. The human agent is part of the ordered cosmos and is indeed that cosmos writ small, a microcosm. He shares characteristics with the inanimate – he can be weighed like a rock; and with the vegetative – he takes nourishment and reproduces himself; and with the animals, sharing with them sense perception and the emotions that follow on them. Of course he is not the only thing in the cosmos that acts. Everything acts and to act is to pursue an end. Thomas accepts and endorses Aristotle's statement at the outset of the *Ethics* that the good is the end that all things seek. Teleology is not then a unique feature of human agents as if they were somehow inserted in a mechanistic universe from which final cause has been eliminated. Under the influence of natural science, philosophers since Kant have seen a chasm between nature and human action. Thomas by contrast sees human action as a special case of a universal fact insofar as it is undertaken for the sake of an end. What is unique to the human agents is that they are free and thus answerable for what they do. It is the good known by intellect that is the object of will. These two faculties or capacities generate voluntary action, either as the act of will itself, elicited voluntary action, or the acts of other capacities insofar as these come under the sway of reasoned will, commanded acts. Human acts and moral acts are identical.

As a microcosm a person is the source of actions that are not moral. Thus many activities are attributed to a person that are not specifically human. Digesting and growing, or shrinking, are truly affirmed of a person, but these are not peculiar to him, nor are they as such amenable to the direction of reason. They are not voluntary. The same must be said of acts of perception and the appetitive responses to what is perceived – desire for the pleasurable and retreat from the menacing are not peculiar to human agents, nor are they voluntary. They simply occur. But unlike vegetative activities they are susceptible of rational and voluntary direction. We may not command our emotions but we are answerable for the choices we make when under their influence.

While it is easy to agree that our emotions just occur involuntarily and thus do not qualify as human acts, it is difficult to see why golfing and carpentry and mowing the lawn do not qualify as human acts, yet it would be a stretch to classify them as moral. They are appraised, of course; one can do them well or badly, but the criteria of the appraisal are hardly moral. A good golfer has to put his mind to it and act voluntarily, but calling him a good golfer is not a moral appraisal. What then of Thomas's identification of human acts and moral acts?

There can be little doubt that human acts can be appraised in a non-moral way, call it a technical appraisal. But such appraisals do not go to the heart of what is going on when one golfs. The fact is that golfing is subject to a moral appraisal as well. One may drive stolen balls, lie about his score, and ignore his obligations to his family as he tramps the fairways. For all that, he may have all the requisite skills and qualify as a good golfer. But it is a commonplace that one can be a good golfer and a bad man or, more likely, a good man and a bad golfer. A moral appraisal is always relevant to any human act but only some of them come under such technical appraisals. And even when they do that is never the full story about them. So the identification of human acts and moral acts stands.

38

Ultimate End in Aristotle

The claim that every human act is undertaken for the sake of an end is compatible with the fact that each act has its own end. Thus the general statement may be true but does not seem to be tantamount to the claim that there is some end for the sake of which we do whatever we do. Yet Thomas, like Aristotle, and indeed the whole classical tradition of morality, holds that there is an ultimate end for the sake of which any action is undertaken. If the claim that there is an ultimate end were simply the fallacious conversion of the proposition "every act is undertaken for the sake of an end" to "there is some end for the sake of which every action is undertaken," it would of course be a risible tenet. But neither Aristotle nor St Thomas maintain that there is an ultimate end on that basis, though they are regularly accused of this. How does Thomas defend the claim?

It would be impossible to enumerate the goals of all the particular human acts that have been, are being, and will be performed. They are unimaginably diverse. Still, it is possible to cluster acts and see that the ends of some are further ordered to the ends of others. In the military, we can distinguish the end for which those in the infantry act from the ends aimed at by those in the artillery, the motor pool, the tank corps, etc. Nonetheless, all these ends are subordinate to the overall point of having an army, defending the community, and fighting against hostile forces with an eye to victory. So too the aim of bricklayers differs from that of glaziers, plumbers, steamfitters, and painters. Yet all these ends can be subordinated to the end of getting a house built. It is this clustering, not some simple fallacy, that leads Aristotle to ask if there is some end for the sake of which all human acts are performed. His affirmative answer is based on a *reductio ad absurdum*.

If, then, there is some end of the things we do, which we desire for its own sake (everything else being desired for the sake of this), and if we do not choose everything for the sake of something else (for at that rate the process would go on to infinity, so that our desire would be empty and vain), clearly this must be the good and the chief good. (*Ethics* I.2. 1094a18–22)

In this translation the passage seems to be merely hypothetical, saying what is meant by ultimate end rather than claiming there is one. That is not how Thomas read it. "First, he shows from what has already been said that there is some best end in human affairs" (*Ethics* I.2, n. 19).

He goes on to show that the passage from Aristotle just cited is a proof that there is an ultimate end.

He uses three arguments, the chief of which is this. *Whatever end is such that we desire other things for its sake and desire it for itself alone and not for any further end, is not only a good end but the best.* This is clear from the fact that any end for the sake of which other ends are sought is the principal end, as is clear from the earlier discussion. *But there must be such an end of human affairs. Therefore, there is some good and best end in human affairs.* (Ibid.)

The assertion that there is such an ultimate end of human actions occurs here as the minor premiss. Of course we want to know if that is true. How is it proved?

He proves the minor by an argument leading to an impossibility, which is this. It is manifest from what was said earlier that one end is sought for the sake of another. Now either this leads to an end which is not desired for something further, or not. If it does, our point is made. If however there should not be found such an end, it would follow that every end is desired for the sake of another end, and this on to infinity. But such an infinity of ends is impossible. Therefore there must be some end which is not sought for the sake of any other end. (Ibid., n. 20)

The nature of this proof is noteworthy. Showing that the denial of a claim leads to absurdity does not of course establish the truth of the original claim. But such a *reductio* is the only proof possible when the very starting points and principles of a discipline are called into question. And it is a feature of such principles that they are *per se nota*, self-evident. Aristotle's procedure here, as explained by Thomas, would seem to entail that the existence of an ultimate end is an inescapable truth of human action. If so, the objections brought against it, and they are many, must be open to the same kind of refutation. But let us go on.

The *reductio* which establishes the truth of the original argument's minor premiss by showing that its denial leads to an impossibility itself involves a claim that requires support. How do we know that there cannot be an infinite regress in ends? This question is a version of another: how do we know that life is not at bottom absurd? The response is that it would be absurd to think so. Why? If one end is sought for the sake of another and that for the sake of another and every end is sought for some further end, action would always be frustrated because it could not terminate in something but always come to something sought for a yet further end. That cannot be because the desire for the good is natural and a natural desire cannot be empty and void. To say so would be to say that the author of nature can be frustrated (n. 21).

It will seem somewhat disarming to be told that the existence of an ultimate end is an inescapable fact of human life. Philosophers have vied with one another to find fault with this claim. The appeal of the third stage of the argument to God, the author of nature, seems to make the starting point of the moral life depend on theism and that would, alas, be enough to put off many. We will see in the sequel that Aristotle and Thomas are indeed right in saying that the ultimate end is an inescapable fact of human action.

39

Ultimate End in Thomas

When one acts he pursues a particular end, a particular good, but implicit in any action is the overall good of the agent. I do not act simply to assuage my thirst or build a wall or defend my family, all particular goods, but because each of these is seen as conducive to what is good for me *tout court*. The good is an umbrella under which the particular goods fall. To desire anything one must see it as a good.

This good functions as the end or purpose that first comes to mind and one then seeks means of attaining it. After such deliberation one may pursue the means which bring one success in attaining the end. Yuri, a young man, becomes enamored of a young woman, Anastasia. He is convinced that life without her would be empty, and resolves to make her his wife. We do not need the complications of the Capulets and Montagues in order that the path before him be not smooth. There are obstacles in his way that must be removed. Our fiction employs this situation again and again. The course of true love never runs smooth, the lover must win his beloved against seemingly insurmountable odds and win through to victory by his own efforts. Stories clarify what in real life is often obscured in a sea of contingency but is nonetheless there. Yuri begins his campaign and after months and months of scenes it would be a delight to narrate finally folds Anastasia in his arms and makes her his own. He has achieved his end. In intention, it was present from the first: it was what he set out to accomplish. In execution, it comes last, but from first to last what he does is intelligible in terms of that end or objective. Not even the so-called *acte gratuit*, the seemingly unmotivated deeds of a Camus hero, escape this, as we shall see.

Now winning Anastasia is Yuri's objective but is marrying her his ultimate end? True, in the elation of young love he will vow to do whatever he does for the sake of his beloved. She has become the purpose of his life. We may imagine him assessing every course of action in terms of what it will do to enhance or diminish his relations with Anastasia. For all that, there was life before Anastasia and he may be forced to face this valley of tears without her some day. Did he have before or will he acquire later a new ultimate end? Attaining his beloved's assent is the fulfillment of his desire. He may think that it is the fulfillment of his every desire and then indeed his happy nuptials will function as his end of ends. What more could he desire?

The ultimate end is just that, the complete fulfillment or perfection of the agent. Thomas suggests that since anything is sought under the aegis of the good, *sub ratione boni*, what is sought is either ultimate or a constituent of the ultimately fulfilling good. This will seem quite formal because it is. So too when Aristotle argues for there being an ultimate end he does so at the beginning of a work that spells out what concretely that end is for the human agent. That there is an ultimate end of human action is an absolute requirement of its being reasonable. But what is our ultimate fulfillment? In what does happiness consist? That is a further question. This is why Thomas can say both that there is the same ultimate end for us all and that we seek it in different places. This is clear when he asks whether there is the same ultimate end for all human agents.

> I reply that it must be said that we can speak of ultimate end in two ways, either according to the notion of ultimate end or in terms of that in which this notion is thought to be realized. With respect to the notion of ultimate end everyone seeks it because everyone seeks to achieve his perfection which is what ultimate end means, as has been said. But with respect to that in which this notion is thought to be realized men are not in agreement, for some seek wealth as the consummate end, some pleasure, some other things. (*ST*, IaIIae, q. 1, a. 7)

This is like saying that all men inescapably seek to be happy but they seek it in wildly different ways. That in fact is the way the point is usually made. Who does not do whatever he does in the expectation that it will make him happy? The task of moral philosophy is to find that which can truly function as our ultimate end. This will turn out to be an ordered amalgam rather than some single thing like Anastasia.

40

Virtuous Action

Man as microcosm sums up the drives and desires found in other and lesser things and he is characterized by intellect and will, thanks to which he aims at his overall good, the ultimate end. Aristotle approaches this through what may be called the function argument. The end or good of any process is what makes it intelligible and provides a criterion for appraising it. Digesting is a process and knowing its purpose enables us to tell whether it is functioning well or badly. So too with seeing or hearing. Once we know the point of a function (*ergon, opus*) we are able to anchor appraisals of it, speak of it as well or badly done. If this is so then, if we can isolate the human function, we will have a basis for speaking of human action as done well or badly. What is the human function? What distinguishes the human agent from all others is that he acts rationally. And there we would seem to have our answer. The good for man is the virtue or perfection of rational activity. Virtue here means simply that the function is performed well; of course it is a notion that becomes central to moral philosophy.

Thanks to Peter Geach in his essay "Good and Evil," and Bernard Williams in his little book *Morality*, the force of this way of identifying the good is once more seen, rescuing moral philosophy from the intuitionism of G. E. Moore's *Principia Ethica* and a whole subsequent tradition of progressively more obscure accounts. It was simply wrong to think that good could be understood apart from the point of the process called good. When we are told by the wily salesman that a car is good we assume that he means that the purposes of a car are fulfilled by this one. If when we drive out of the lot, the wheels come off, the doors become unhinged, and the engine falls to the street, we will rightly think we have been misled. If the salesman is G. E. Moore he will try to tell us that he had none of those things in mind in calling the car good. Nor any other such factual characteristics of the vehicle. Value judgments float free of any natural properties of the thing. Goodness is something we just see, like yellow. We in turn will see red. We are unlikely to accept such nonsense, however long a career the theory had among philosophers. To call something good is to say that it fulfills well the purpose for which it was made.

One can see the rightness of the function account of the good without agreeing that it leads on to clarity as to what the ultimate purpose of human life is. Williams, for example, having resumed and strengthened Geach's argument, sadly concludes that the function argument cannot take us to where Aristotle thought it did. Among his reasons are that despoiling the environment is something only rational animals do and that robbing banks requires rational activity. Such objections are unworthy of Williams. They assume that deliberately fouling our ecological nest and robbing banks successfully are instances of good rational activity. Obviously further inquiry is needed to show that such objections do not tell against what Thomas and Aristotle proposed as that which does indeed fulfill the notion of ultimate end.

If the peculiar characteristic of man is rational activity, and if the good performance, or virtue, of rational activity is what enables us to call a man good, much as a good golfer is one who golfs well, it is nonetheless quickly clear that rational activity is of several kinds.

There is the activity of reason as such, whose perfection is truth; there is the perfection of reason as guiding and directing other faculties to the overall good of the person – of course they have natural ends of their own – and such activities other than reason, such as choosing, fearing, desiring, can be called rational insofar as they come under the sway of practical reason. So there are three great categories of rational activity: theoretical reasoning, practical reasoning, and participated rationality. On this basis, we would have to say that there are three kinds of virtue involved in designating the human agent good. Much of the task of moral philosophy and moral theology is spelling out the specific kinds of these generic virtues, as is clear from the procedure of the *Nicomachean Ethics* and the second part of the *Summa Theologiae*. And Thomas like Aristotle will argue that this is an ordered set of virtues, such that some more perfectly fulfill the human agent than others. We will return to this.

It is clear that moral philosophy for Thomas is a reflection on how we can act well, how we can achieve the end we naturally desire, call it happiness. The moral task is to acquire a character which enables us to maneuver through the contingencies of life in such a way that we act well and thus achieve what is perfective of us. The desire for the good is a given, that is what is meant by calling it natural. However, reflection not only reveals the notion of ultimate end, but makes clear that we must do those things which truly constitute our fulfillment and perfection. The criteria for the true good must be sought in our nature as rational agents. How do we go about finding the true guidelines for our actions?

41

Natural Law

The moral task is one of schooling ourselves to judge correctly as to what is fulfilling of us and to pursue it. This is a task that gradually dawns upon us and we have been around for quite a while before it does. In those so-to-speak pre-moral years our lives are sustained and guided by our parents and we come under the influence of the society into which we happen to have been born. We do not choose our parents or the time in which our lives are lived or the cultural ambience that surrounds us. We unquestioningly, at least at first, accept the guidance given us and much of its influence goes unnoticed. The rewards and punishments of our upbringing instill criteria for appraising what is good or bad for us to do. The music we hear, the games we play, the television programs we are allowed to see, playmates, teachers – all these too shape us before we can shape ourselves. And of course such upbringing may be wrong- or right-headed. A time comes when we responsibly accept or reject that moral education. What are the criteria for the one or the other?

Moral education inculcates ways of regarding certain things as fulfilling of us and others as frustrating our desire to be happy. Any moral education can be seen as proposing certain actions as fulfilling of the assumed desire for fulfillment or perfection. Moral philosophy begins, not in a conceptual void, but in such particular ways of seeing good and evil. Some have spoken of moral traditions to point to this fact, lest we think that "issues from the hand of God the simple soul," untrammeled by upbringing, uninfluenced by cultural surroundings. But the moral task begins when we responsibly adopt or reject the assumptions of the tradition in which we have been born and raised. Thomas's remarkable treatment of what he calls natural law elaborates the criteria for such appraisal.

A first definition of natural law is that it is the peculiarly human participation in God's provident direction of creation. Call this the theological or metaphysical definition. It assumes a cosmos in which the good is that which all things seek and where human agents, who share many drives and desires with lesser agents, are distinguished by the fact that they are to direct themselves knowingly and willingly to that which is fulfilling of their nature.

A second definition of natural law is that it consists of the first guiding principles of action which are lodged in what we are. Knowing how we are to act, making judgments which guide our choices and decisions, practical knowing, can be compared with theoretical knowing, and that is what Thomas does in the famous text analyzed earlier in chapter 13.

Knowing, as we have seen, is to grasp the form of another as other and to make true affirmations and denials about natures. This is intellectual knowing in the basic sense and its perfection lies in its truth: this is the perfection of the knowing process as such. Practical knowing is an extension of this, and is had when our goal is not simply to know but to guide and direct activities other than knowing. The first criterion, then, for distinguishing the theoretical from the practical use of our mind is the end in view, the perfection of knowing as such or the perfection of some activity other than knowing, e.g. willing (*On the Soul*, III.10). In order to accommodate the fact that there are degrees of these two kinds of knowing, Thomas adds two other criteria, object and method. The proper objects of knowing as such, theoretical knowing, are things that we do not make or bring about by our actions. The objects of practical knowing are such things, do-ables and make-ables. But we can think about such objects in the way in which we think of natural things, classifying and comparing, as we might define a house as a kind of shelter against the elements and, to distinguish it from umbrellas and tents, add that it is a fixed structure, walled, roofed, heated, etc. This is the same method that a botanist might employ in expressing what a snapdragon is. The practical way of knowing make-able or do-able things is to know how to bring them about, as a recipe in a cookbook provides knowledge which brings into being a pineapple upsidedown cake. Natural things can be known in only one way, but do-able things, actions, say, can be defined as natural events as well as known in an action-guiding way. The third criterion is the end of the knowing, already discussed (*ST*, Ia, q. 14, a. 16).

There are, accordingly, three levels of practical knowledge. (1) We might know make-able and do-able things in the way in which we know natural things and then our end is simply to obtain the truth about them. Call this *minimally practical knowledge*. (2) We might know make-able and do-able things as the result of a series of acts to be performed: digging a foundation, raising the walls, installing the roof beam, tiling the roof, bricking the outside walls, etc. Architectural students might talk thus about a possible structure they are not presently engaged in constructing. Call this *virtually practical knowledge*. (3) Finally, we might be cognitively concerned with the do-able, know it in a way that brings about an action, and indeed be engaged in performing that action. Call this *completely practical knowledge*.

Completely practical knowledge is embedded in the performance of particular acts. It is always singular since actions are singular. But such knowledge brings to bear on the project general knowledge, as the fledgling architect may go on to build the edifice he has been designing in class, making virtually practical knowledge completely practical knowledge. Virtually practical knowledge is action-guiding but it can be remote or proximate to the actual doing. Moral philosophy is on the level of generality and involves more or less general action-guiding knowledge. It will also include minimally practical knowledge, as when virtue is defined, and species of virtue.

There is a kind of practical knowing of great generality, so general that it is presupposed by moral philosophy as such. This is the level on which the principles of natural law are found. Because practical knowing is an extension of theoretical knowing, Thomas approaches the discussion of these first principles by developing an analogy between theoretical and practical knowing. The starting points of knowledge are had by natural operations, ones that do not await our decision to come about. Merely the formulation of the notion, however vague, of the good, of our fulfillment, suffices to provide an object the will cannot not desire. We are not free to desire happiness, we desire it willy-nilly. Thomas thinks it helps us to consider the procedure of theoretical knowing first.

There are two acts of intellect, one by which we grasp what things are, which is expressed in accounts or definitions, and another expressed in affirmations and denials. In both cases there is a first that comes naturally. In the case of the first operation of intellect, being is the first concept formed. "Being is the first thing apprehended, and an understanding of it is included in whatever else is grasped" (*ST* IaIIae, q. 94, a. 2). Anything of which we form a concept is grasped as a being. Being is latent in any other concept, so that when we find in our baby book that our first word was "hot" this is an illustration of the claim rather than a counterexample to it. It is some hot thing or being that dawned on our infant mind. Obviously it would be surprising to find "being" listed as one's first utterance. If that were the claim, it would strike us as, well, philosophical. Thomas's point is that we know whatever kind of thing we first know as being, albeit a being of a given kind. But precision only reveals that we are moving within the ambience of the-things-that-are, being. As Thomas puts it, being is implicit in every other concept. That is the sense in which being is the first thing naturally known.

There is also a first judgment, indemonstrable and self-evident: "It is impossible for something to be and not to be at the same time and in the same respect." Now this is not a sentence uttered even by the children of philosophers until far along in their linguistic history. The point is that this judgment, like the grasp of being, is implicit in any judgment that we make. When children argue as to who struck the first blow, there is an exchange of "You did!" "I didn't!" You did!" I didn't!" And on and on until the paternal or maternal parent inter-venes. These childish disputants are in heated disagreement, but on one thing they are manifestly agreed. If the first child struck the first blow then the second did not and vice versa. Without an underlying agreement, argument would be impossible. But of course children recognize that someone either did or did not start the fight and embedded in that realization, and in any other affirmation, is that the affirmation and its denial cannot be simultaneously true.

With this recalled, Thomas develops the parallel in the practical use of our mind. Here too there is something first grasped, the good, some-thing known as desirable. Children do use "good" early on, even though they are unlikely to use "being." And there is a first practical judgment as well: the good ought to be pursued and done and evil avoided. This first practical judgment is the basic precept of natural law.

What Thomas is describing here as first principles of the theoret-ical and practical orders are pre-philosophical. This is the kind of knowledge everyone already has, the truth of which is presupposed by the reflective and increasingly sophisticated discourse of philoso-phy. There are certain truths everyone can be presumed to know prior to the study of philosophy and to which appeal is made by the philosopher as to something requiring no proof. Of course, as in the text we are analyzing, the philosopher reflects on and clarifies this pre-philosophical knowledge and the tyro may be surprised that he has been speaking prose all along, as it were. But these are not truths one learns in philosophy: rather, he sees that he has known them all along, however implicitly.

42

Natural Inclinations

Is this first principle the only precept of natural law or are there others that can be recognized as non-gainsayable, in need of no proof other than a *reductio*? Thomas goes on to provide the basis for the formulation of other natural law precepts which presuppose and thus are based upon the first, that good should be done and evil avoided. His general rule is this:

> On this are based all other precepts of natural law, such that other things to be done or avoided pertain to natural law which practical reason naturally apprehends to be human goods. Because good has the character of end and evil is its contrary, reason naturally apprehends as good all those things to which men have a natural inclination, and consequently as things to be pursued; their contraries are perceived as evils to be avoided. The order of the precepts of natural law is based on the order of natural inclinations. (*ST* IaIIae, q. 94, a. 2)

There is a first precept of natural law which is implicit in all practical judgments and there are other judgments of what is to be done and avoided which, like the first principle, are indemonstrable. These secondary precepts of natural law form a hierarchy which is based on the hierarchy of natural inclinations. Inclinations are called natural because we have them whether we wish to or not, they are facts of our nature. What are these natural inclinations? There is first an inclination which men share with all things insofar as all things seek to preserve themselves in being. There is, next, an inclination to more special things which men share with the other animals – sexual union of the genders, the raising of young, etc. Finally, there is an inclination peculiar to man to know the truth about God and to live in society.

These inclinations are not as such precepts of natural law, but that on which precepts for guiding action are based. Precepts of natural law are the formulation of action-guiding principles based on the inclinations. Precepts having to do with the consumption of food and drink, which preserve us in being, will be concerned with how to conduct ourselves vis-à-vis the pleasures of food and drink. On the second inclination will be based judgments as to how sexual union and its results should be rationally governed. The specifically human inclination will give rise to action-guiding principles for the pursuit of knowledge and living with others. It is perhaps noteworthy that Thomas does not formulate these principles, but they would doubtless look like this. Food and drink ought to be pursued in a way conducive to our overall good. Sexual activity should be engaged in a way that takes into account what it is, what its purpose is, and which should be conducive to our overall good. And so too with precepts based on the third inclination. The idea is that a judgment that food and drink ought to be pursued night and day, with no eye to the point of taking nourishment or to our overall well-being, is not one that could reasonably be maintained. So too the pell-mell pursuit of sexual pleasure with man or beast could scarcely be thought of as conducive to our overall well-being. The very sweeping generality of such principles is a condition of their being beyond argument. They establish the parameters of moral discourse. Ever more concrete judgments of how we should behave in these areas will require rational support and are likely to be true only for the most part. And that is a sign that they are not precepts of natural law. It is from moral philosophy that we expect this elucidation of how we ought to act, but this is undertaken against the background of presupposed truths everyone may be expected to know and which brood over moral theory.

43

Virtue and Law

Earlier we spoke of the moral life as the task of forming a character such that we do well in the fleeting and altering circumstances of life, seeking the means to achieve the end we desire. Is that account at odds with the moral life spoken of in terms of a hierarchy of precepts? Thomas clearly doesn't think so and there are many texts in which he fuses the two analyses. Thus, when discussing the object naturally desired by will, he says this:

> This is the good in general to which the will naturally tends, as any other power tends to its object, and also the ultimate end which functions in desirable things as the first principles of demonstration do in things to be understood, and generally everything befitting the one willing because of his nature. We do not in using our will seek only what pertains to the faculty of will but also what pertains to the other powers and to the whole man. Hence a man not only naturally loves the object of will but also what pertains to the other powers, such as

knowledge of the true, which pertains to intellect, and to be and to live and other such things which pertain to our natural makeup, all of which fall under the object of will as particular goods. (Ibid., q. 10, a. 1)

Philosophers after Thomas divorced duty and nature, value and fact, and tried to talk about moral duty as divorced from our desire for happiness and to maintain that judgments that a thing is good have nothing to do with what the thing is. The passage just quoted may suffice to show how for Thomas the desire for happiness, the love of the good, is part and parcel of the action-guiding judgments that he calls precepts of natural law.

44

Practical Syllogism

Natural law provides the first self-evident principles of practical discourse. Moral philosophy is a reflection on the demands of action carried on at a level of greater or lesser universality. But actions are singular and may be seen as the application of such general knowledge to the concrete case. Indeed, the thinking we are engaged in as we act here and now is called by Thomas a practical syllogism. In this he is following Aristotle's lead when the philosopher is confronting the great puzzle bequeathed to him by Plato: is bad action the consequence of ignorance and acting well a necessary consequence of knowing the good? Is knowing what we ought to do tantamount to doing it?

Two distinctions are required for any adequate answer to this question. First, a distinction between knowing in general what one should do and knowing here and now, in this case, what I should do. Second, a distinction between having knowledge and actually using it. The sleeping surgeon is called a surgeon because he could, if roused, wield his scalpel, but now he is simply snoozing. His knowledge too sleeps, as it were, but it can be wakened.

With these distinctions in hand, Aristotle remarks that it would be odd to think that someone actually thinking of the good he should do here and now should act contrary to that knowledge; the knowledge is embedded in his action, he is in effect acting on that knowledge. On the other hand, surely there is nothing odd about saying that someone can know that fasting allays concupiscence without ever acting on that ascetic principle, and that when he does act he still knows it but isn't thinking of it.

The practical syllogism, which will emerge as an account of what rationality means in the practical sphere, is first introduced to see what goes wrong when someone possessed of true moral principles fails to abide by them in the crunch. The assumption is that the person is drawn to the good that he knows; the general principles are not simply truths but truths about that which draws and engages the will. He wants to become temperate. He leaves the lecture hall aglow with idealism. In his mind's eye his future self appears as a model of moderation and temperance. And then a voice calls out to him as he passes an open door over which is engraved Den of Iniquity. The siren call is repeated. He enters, slips onto a bar stool, and the first of many drinks is put before him. Much later, reeling with remorse, he goes home.

We can all replace such facetious examples with examples from our own experience of such failures of will. How analyze these moral failures? They are not due to lack of knowledge. The agent knows full well how he should act and indeed how he desires to act. There is no need to doubt his sincerity. But who among us has not fallen short of his moral ideal, betrayed it, acted contrary to it? Original sin, we might say, and of course that is true, however remote an explanation of this lapse. Our thinking when we act can be seen as involving general knowledge of what we should do, as a major premiss, and the assessment of our here-and-now circumstances in the light of the general knowledge, as minor premiss, and, as conclusion, the action. The minor premiss is where things can go wrong. When you succumbed and entered the Den of Iniquity you were acting knowingly although not on the knowledge with which you left the lecture all aglow. The familiar garish entrance to the Den exerts its attraction and when you go inside for a night of debauchery the general principle you are acting under is: never pass up the chance to get drunk in wicked and congenial surroundings. This is the principle, though not even you would state it aloud, that expresses what functions as your good, that is, what really attracts you, where your heart is. This is why more than a crackerjack lecture on temperance is going to be required if you are to become temperate.

You must change your heart. Only by dint of repeated acts, performed with difficulty and against the grain, will temperance become your good such that acting in accord with it in changing circumstances is merely a matter of your acting in character.

45

End/Means

Thomas offers another and complementary analysis of action in terms of end and means. This of course follows quite naturally from discussions of ultimate end. How is it to be achieved? Thomas distinguishes three acts of will which bear on the end. There is, first, the will's response to knowledge of the good, a response which is called by the name of the power because it is so basic (*voluntas*). Further dwelling on it is such that one takes pleasure in the thought of the good (*fruitio*) and may be drawn on to wanting the good as an object of pursuit (*intentio*). With the rise of intention, one begins to think how the good or end can be realized. All acts of will are consequent on cognition, of course, but the search for means to the end, deliberation, gets a special discussion. Deliberation may turn up more than one way to achieve the end, any one of which has its charms; one consents to them (*consensus*) but must choose among them, or, if there be but one, choose it (*electio*). All this is in the order of deliberation. Then the order of execution begins and the will makes use of the other powers to move the agent toward the end (*usus*).

Of course Thomas does not imagine that we go reflectively through all these stages every time we act, but he does think they are implicit in anything we do. And of course there are times when they become fully conscious and reflective moments of an action. When Trollope's *Ralph the Heir* sets about the task of proposing marriage to a young woman, something he does three times in the course of the novel, his decision is fully deliberate and can be shown to illustrate the analysis Thomas has given.

But the surest way we have to see that these stages are implicit in any action is when the act is aborted. We might find our will drawn to something recognized as good and that is the end of it. There are so many such things in any case that we could scarcely get involved with them all. But we might dwell on the possible (for us) good and take pleasure in the thought; thus, there are sins of thought and virtues too of a sort. But no intention to go for the good in the thought of which we take pleasure might follow, nor given the intention do we necessarily go on to deliberate about the means of achieving it, but we might, and like what we come up with, yet not choose it. In this way, by noticing how acts can be incomplete in various degrees, the constituents of the complete act are verified.

The end/means analysis of action and the analysis in terms of the practical syllogism are complementary ones, as the remark that deliberation is the search for the minor premiss of the practical syllogism suggests.

46

The Common Good

Influenced as we doubtless are by theories developed after Thomas, we are likely to think of ourselves as isolated individuals such that the desire for the good or for happiness may seem restricted to my private good. Following Aristotle, Thomas recognizes three kinds of moral science: ethics, economics and politics. Politics is the controlling wisdom in the practical order such that concern for the shared good of the domestic community (economics) and the integral goodness of the individual agent must seem abstract and torn from the context in which we act. The human good is the good of humans as they actually are. But to be a human is to be born into a family; there is no way we can get into the world apart from the activity of our forebears. (Even if a bottle instead of a womb is our primordial dwelling, as in *Brave New World*, lab workers must act *in loco paren-*

tis, so to say.) So too Aristotle's famous remark that man is by nature a political animal does not mean that as isolated individuals we have a tendency to get together and write constitutions. We are naturally political in the sense that we are born into a society, into a family. That is what it is to be a human. Consequently, any talk of the human good has to be talk of what is good for humans as we find them. This is why the shared good, whether of the family or of the polis, is more our good than is our merely private good. There will be some virtues appropriate to our private good – for example, courage and temperance – others to our actions as children (piety) and as spouses (fidelity), and yet others to our actions as citizens. Far from being a metaphor, civic virtue is the noblest perfection of practical man.

What then of the claim that the virtues of that rational activity which is the theoretical use of our mind most fully and perfectly perfect us as rational agents since they perfect what is most characteristic of us? And what of the notorious and connected Aristotelian claim that contemplation, which can only be thought of in relation to metaphysics, is the chief good of man and that in which our happiness primarily consists, a view concurred in by Thomas? The pursuit of theoretical truth and the contemplation of it will seem like the most singular, even private, activities. And if even the political virtues are subordinate to it, we seem to be led to the conclusion that the whole organization of a well-ordered society is aimed at the private activities of an intellectual elite.

Thomas's answer to this is that contemplation bears on the most shareable good of all, one that far from being diminished by being shared is meant to be as widely shared as possible. Moreover, the culminating object of knowledge is knowledge of God who is the common good of the entire universe. However singular your acts of contemplation may be they relate you to the good toward which everything in the universe and every human being tends. Furthermore, no one could lead a life exclusively of contemplation. Contemplation is, as it were, episodic even in a life defined principally by it. The contemplative is a man for all that, and is embedded in the community of which he is a member and which continues to make its claims on him. Finally, contemplation, which Aristotle discusses in Book Ten of the *Ethics,* is the activity which fuses the moral and the theoretical.

47

Natural and Supernatural Ends

How can Thomas Aquinas, a Christian, possibly agree with Aristotle on the ultimate point of human life? Surely the pagan view of happiness, however exalted it be, falls far short of the happiness promised the believer in the next life. Nonetheless, Thomas explains and defends the views of Aristotle as he comments on the *Nicomachean Ethics* and in his incomplete commentary on the *Politics*. Is this a case of scholarly schizophrenia? Or perhaps an indication that in such commentaries Thomas is not endorsing or accepting what he finds so much as making the best case for it that he can?

This is no small problem. Jacques Maritain, one of the most eminent Thomists of the twentieth century, maintained that moral philosophy divorced from revelation simply could not achieve the status of a practical science. Original sin, redemption, and a call to an end beyond anything we could naturally expect, render a merely philosophical ethics like Aristotle's unreal. Unless it is supplemented by, and indeed subalternated to moral theology, it is going to be radically defective. One gets no sense of this attitude in reading Thomas's commentary on the *Ethics*.

There is of course a superficial way in which Aristotle and Thomas could be said to be in agreement on man's ultimate end. They both have the same notion of ultimate end, the *ratio ultimi finis*, and thus could be said to posit the same ultimate end in the way that all men are said to have the same ultimate end. The difference would then lie in the fact that Aristotle sees that notion realized in one way and Thomas in another.

The question then becomes: what is the nature of the difference between Aristotle's notion of what realizes the ultimate end, where happiness is concretely to be found, and that of St Thomas Aquinas? Is it a case of H and –H, that is, of two contradictorily opposed claims as to the way the notion of happiness is realized? But it is just this sense of contradictory opposition that seems utterly absent from Thomas's treatment of Aristotle's moral philosophy, whether in the commentary or in his theological writings. Aristotle is invoked as an ally, as an invaluable source of light on such questions as the ultimate end, virtue, justice, prudence, and contemplation. Aquinas does not demur when Aristotle defines happiness as a life lived according to virtue and, when he arrays the virtues hierarchically as constituents of that happiness, gives pride of place to contemplation. Whenever Thomas discusses such moral matters, Aristotle is invoked. The moral part of the *Summa Theologiae* begins with five questions on the ultimate end and happiness whose dependence on the *Ethics* is obvious. So how did Thomas reconcile the philosophical or pagan conception of happiness with the Christian?

We owe to Aristotle the articulation of the notion of ultimate end. This notion of ultimate end or happiness is flawless, so far as Thomas is concerned. But what then of Aristotle's views as to where it is realized? Thomas has obviously been on the lookout when reading Aristotle to see if the philosopher thought that what he puts forward as truly realizing the notion of ultimate end is meant to be an exhaustive account. Is it meant to be the last word because it completely realizes the concept of ultimate end? Obviously if Aristotle thought this, Thomas would be bound to disagree with him. But he finds in Aristotle a recognition that what he is putting forward only imperfectly realizes the notion of ultimate end. Several times in the course of the discussion at the outset of the IaIIae he cites a text from Book One of the *Ethics* (1101a20), in which Aristotle says that of course he is speaking of what we men can expect to achieve. Thomas takes this to be the admission that what Aristotle teaches only imperfectly realizes the notion of ultimate end. Of course, he could have invoked many other passages where it is clear that our ability to do the things that constitute happiness is limited and episodic. One need only think of Aristotle's discussion of contemplation in *Ethics X*. Aristotle clearly did not think that we are able to achieve a life which exhausts once and for all the notion of ultimate end. If nothing else, there is always the possibility of misfortune crushing us and making the moral task stale or even impossible.

By contrast, Thomas as a Christian believer accepts the promise of a perfect realization of happiness, indeed a realization that goes beyond a happiness commensurate with our nature. But, in the oft-repeated adage, the supernatural does not destroy nature but perfects it. This is nowhere more obvious than in Thomas's theology in which natural knowledge becomes part of a wider whole defined by revelation. So too in his moral theology, moral philosophy is a component. And that is the basis for Thomas's resolution of the question we have posed.

There is but one true understanding of what the ultimate end is, the *ratio felicitatis*. Aristotle and Thomas are agreed on that. There is a realization of ultimate end which, however noble it is, is imperfect, human all too human. Aristotle and Thomas are agreed that the philosophical account of ultimate end is imperfect. However, Thomas holds that there is a perfect realization of the notion of ultimate end, albeit in the next world, but that is where we're heading. Thus he will speak of perfect and imperfect happiness and even of a twofold ultimate end, meaning two ways of realizing it. The imperfect is true as far as it goes and that is why it can be subsumed into moral theology.

48

Preambles of Faith

The way in which Thomas puts together the truths of philosophy and the truths known by revelation in moral theology, is but a special case of his teaching on the relationship between philosophy and theology. We have seen that Thomas holds that it is possible to arrive at knowledge of God and of some of his attributes quite independently of religious belief. This possibility has been realized by pagan philosophers, and is not put forward simply as logically possible. Revelation contains truths about God which could never have been guessed by the most inquiring philosopher since the world around us cannot lead us to them as it can lead to knowledge that God exists.

Are there then two different sets of truths about God, those knowable by our natural powers and those knowable only on the basis of faith? In some sense that is the case, but it will occur to us that the truths about God that the philosopher can know are among the truths the believer believes. God exists is presupposed by belief that he is triune or became incarnate in Jesus. It seems inescapable that the truths about God said to be naturally knowable have also been revealed. This leads Thomas to make a distinction among revealed truths. Most of them are *mysteries*, that is, truths that could never have been known apart from revelation. But undeniably naturally knowable truths about God are also included in revelation. Thomas proposes that we call these *preambles* of faith.

Why would God reveal truths that can be known by our natural powers? Among the reasons Thomas gives is this. Knowledge of God is the most important thing there is: if God exists, this has decisive significance for the way we live. But philosophical knowledge of God is the culminating achievement of a long and difficult quest. It would be unfortunate if each person had to go through that laborious process before settling an issue that is of supreme importance now. If God does not exist, I will regard the world and myself and what I might or might not do quite differently than if I know that he exists. It is a sign of God's mercy that he enables us to know the answer on the basis of faith, to know it when young, when the knowledge can become part of the warp and woof of our life. The preambles, as revealed, are also purged of the errors that creep into even generally true philosophical accounts of God.

For Thomas, the preambles support the believer's conviction that his acceptance of the mysteries, truths he can only hold on the basis of faith, is reasonable. If some of the things revelation proposes for our acceptance can be known to be true, it is reasonable to think that the mysteries too are intelligible, however mysterious in this life. (Of course the promise is that what is so accepted now will be seen to be true in the next life: faith is not a permanent condition of the mind, and will pass away when one sees even as he is seen.)

49

Christian Philosophy

If the believer already holds true answers to philosophical questions how could he possibly be a philosopher like all others? This question is usually put by those who assume that the philosopher is not a believer or, if he is, that this could not possibly have any relevance to his philosophizing. Sometimes the question suggests that the Christian departs from the norm simply by having antecedent convictions that he brings to philosophy. Since Kierkegaard's lampooning of the Hegelian quest for an absolute starting point for thought, one would think that the inescapability of antecedent convictions would be seen to be, well, inescapable. Everyone brings a lot of baggage with him as he climbs the purgatorial mountain of philosophy. For many it is received opinion that God does not exist, that there are no moral absolutes, that man is fated rather than free, that death is the end, period. I don't mean these as theses analyzed and argued for, but as assumptions that guide the philosopher's choice of topics and do indeed influence his overt discussion of them. Just like the Christian's beliefs.

Is this a mere *tu quoque*? It is rather a reminder of something that is obvious in the case of the believer and somehow unnoticed in the case of the non-believing philosopher. Does this relativize philosophical argument, making it merely a function of our antecedent convictions? Not if there are common criteria for appraising arguments whatever their provenance in antecedent convictions.

We could not end this swift and sketchy presentation of the philosophy of Thomas without adding that for him there is an enormous advantage had when we philosophize within the ambience of the faith. The believer sees his philosophical efforts in the context of his Christian vocation. This does not prevent his seeing the essential difference between arguments based on principles accessible to everyone and arguments based on principles accepted as true on the basis of faith. That is just what Thomas means by the difference between philosophy and theology. The recognition of the autonomy of philosophy, of the formal difference of philosophical arguments, is not incipient apostasy on the believer's part. Indeed, it may be an indication of how seriously he takes what Paul says in Romans 1:20.

50

Beyond Philosophy

The opening article of the *Summa Theologiae* makes clear that beginners in the study of Sacred Doctrine are considered to be already knowledgeable in the philosophical sciences. That familiarity raises a question. How does the theology that is the telos of philosophizing compare with the knowledge of God that comes by way of revelation? In comparing and contrasting the two theologies, Thomas presents each of them in the guise of a science in the Aristotelian mode.

Science as a body of knowledge is made up of arguments which seek new truths about a subject matter, that is, about the subject of the conclusion of a demonstration more or less generically understood, e.g. plane figure, triangle, or isosceles triangle. Such arguments form a single science insofar as their subjects are defined in the same way, e.g. without sensible matter in the case of mathematicals.

In the strongest instance of scientific proof, the apodictic or demonstrative syllogism, the middle term is the definition of the subject and what is proved is a property of the subject, that is, some characteristic it has simply in virtue of being the sort of thing it is. Such arguments or demonstrations are said to be of the reasoned fact (*propter quid*). Since our natural knowledge of God is only oblique, via his effects, arguments establishing that certain things are true of him are called arguments of fact (*quia*). This changes somewhat when revelation comes into play, revelation being a privileged access, God telling us about himself. Accordingly, Thomas's comparison of philosophical theology and the theology based on Sacred Scripture becomes somewhat complicated.

The first contrast has to do with the principles or presuppositions of the two kinds of discourse. Philosophy for Thomas, as we have seen, is ultimately grounded in truths accessible to anyone with standard cognitive equipment. There are certain self-evident truths in the public domain from which the philosopher takes off. We have already noted how this distinguishes philosophy in Thomas's sense of the term – what might be called the classical sense – from all those modern philosophies which begin with doubt or skepticism about any pre-philosophical truth claims. These naturally knowable principles are read off our experience of sensible things and can take us only so far as we can extrapolate from sensible things to non-sensible things. That is why, for the philosopher, knowledge of God is always a function of our knowledge of physical objects, something which, as we have been stressing, is evident in the way in which a terminology which has its native habitat in sensible things is extended to such more than sensible things as can be known on the basis of our knowledge of sensible things. The theology based on Sacred Scripture, supernatural as opposed to natural theology, takes as its starting points truths which have been revealed.

Faith and theology

It is a mark of revealed truths that we cannot *know* them to be true on the basis of our knowledge of sensible things. Natural theology can establish that God exists, that there is only one God, that God is the cause of all else, and other divine attributes which, again, are anchored in our knowledge of the world and ourselves. How can truths about God that we cannot understand in this way, cannot know to be true in this way, be held to be true? The answer is, faith. That God is a trinity of persons in one nature, that Christ is a person with both a divine and human nature, that sins can be forgiven and that we are destined for an eternity of bliss with God, and so forth, cannot be known to be true in any ordinary sense of know. They are believed. Such faith is not an achievement but a gift. It is a grace. The human mind, moved by grace, gives its assent to truths it cannot now understand, on the basis of divine authority, motivated by the promise of eternal happiness. Since these revealed truths, the mysteries of faith, are the principles of supernatural theology, only the believer can engage in such discourse.

But is that true? There are many students of the *Summa Theologiae* who do not share the faith of its author. They may have no religious beliefs whatsoever. Yet their learned and informative articles about the theological works of Thomas appear in respectable journals and are available in better bookstores everywhere. Why then say, as Thomas does, that faith is necessary to engage in theological discourse?

Distinguo. There is of course what might be called a spectator's or scholar's approach to theology. Such a one can tell us how the arguments work, what their presuppositions are, the sources of the doctrine, the validity of the arguments, and many many other things for which we can only be grateful. So what is missing? For such a one, the discourse he is studying is not truth-conveying. The truths we learn from him are historical, textual, philological, but not theological. Only one who accepts the premises as true will find the arguments bringing to light new truths. The scholar, as we have described him, does not sign on to the truths which are the principles and the source of any further truths in theology. The believer, pondering what he accepts as true, is in the Anselmian phrase seeking understanding, seeking to penetrate more deeply the truths he accepts on faith. If those principles are not accepted as true, the learning and scholarship are of a different order, distinct from doing theology, as we might say.

Faith is the presupposition of supernatural theology, not synonymous with it. Not every believer engages in the kind of sophisticated discourse that we find in the *Summa Theologiae*. Furthermore, theological discourse in this sense does not remove the need to take the starting points on faith. The Anselmian phrase, faith seeking understanding, is often applied to supernatural theology, but the kind of understanding achieved never removes the necessity of accepting the starting points on faith. That is, the theologian cannot prove the truth of the Trinity, or of the union of two natures in Christ, or any of the other specific truths of Christianity. Supernatural theology is, thus, not a standard instance of Aristotelian science, however much that model is employed to describe it.

Magister sacrae paginae

The training of the master in theology in the medieval university proceeded on several tracks, one of which was the study of Sacred Scripture. If revealed truths supply the principles of theology and if Sacred Scripture is the means of revelation, a close study of the sacred texts would naturally form the heart of the theologian's work. Thomas's inaugural lecture when he became a master of theology was a commendation of Sacred Scripture accompanied by a rapid survey and ordering of the contents of the Bible. Biblical commentaries form a significant portion of the collected works of Thomas.

Just as Thomas's interpretations of Aristotle were based on Latin translations, so for him the Bible was the Vulgate Latin translation. He had no Greek or Hebrew. His commentaries on Scripture fall naturally into those on books of the Old Testament, and those on books of the New.

In the former category, we have a remarkable commentary on Job, what Thomas called a literal commentary. I was once startled to be told by my colleague Boleslaw Sobocinski, founding editor of the *Notre Dame Journal of Formal Logic*, that he found this commentary on Job a precious source of logical insights. He took the meaning of this remark to his grave, but one need not be a formal logician to savor this commentary on one of the most fascinating books of the Bible. It is noteworthy that there are recent translations of this commentary into English as well as French.

The Psalms were essential to the liturgical prayers of the Church and Thomas, like other priests, recited some of them every day in the Divine Office. He undertook a commentary on the Psalms, completing 54 of the 150. He is said to have commented on the Canticle of Canticles on his deathbed, in response to the request of the Cistercians of Fossanova in whose monastery he died. Alas, no such commentary has come down to us. We do have a commentary on Isaiah, which Thomas wrote in what is called his *litera inintelligibilis* – unreadable hand. It was transcribed by his companion William of Tocco and is largely what was called a cursory reading of the text, an initial explanation but without developing theologically the problems it raised. We have a similar cursory reading of Jeremiah and another on the Lamentations.

Thomas's extant commentaries on books of the New Testament are more numerous and richer in content. There is first of all the self-effacing *Catena Aurea* or *Golden Chain* on the Four Gospels, gleaned from the writing of the Fathers and later authoritative interpreters. Thomas is present only as the gatherer and purveyor of their views. This was one of the first works put into English by members of the Oxford Movement, doubtless because it is a compendium and treasury of centuries of biblical commentary.

Of Thomas's own commentaries on the Gospels, we have two, that on Matthew and that on John. These are *reportationes*, that is, notes on Thomas's lectures, the second by Reginald of Piperno, perhaps Thomas's closest and most devoted Dominican friend. Doubtless the most impressive work in this second category is Thomas's commentary on the epistles of St Paul, again with the assistance of Reginald

of Piperno as reporter, although edited by Thomas himself. In his prologue, Thomas discusses the ordering of the epistles, distinguishing
their chronology – based on internal evidence – from their canonical
ordering. However occasional these letters were, Thomas as commentator finds a doctrinal ordering in them.

Developments in Scripture scholarship for a time led to a devalu-
ing of Thomas's biblical commentaries, but more recently there has
been a growing sense of the value and importance of medieval commentaries in general and in particular those of Thomas Aquinas.
Thomists like Florent Gaboriau have lamented the tendency among
theologians interested in Thomas to slight his biblical commentaries,
but this too seems to be changing. In any case, it is important for an
accurate understanding of Thomas's literary production to give full
weight to this sizeable body of work. Like television preachers of our
own time, Thomas had the Bible at his fingertips and his commentaries are replete with the invocation of other texts to cast light on
the one before him. This is perhaps particularly true of his commentaries on the Pauline epistles.

The three infinitives that summed up the task of the master of
theology – *legere, disputare, praedicare* (to read, dispute and preach)
– assured the centrality of Sacred Scripture. Sermons, of course, drew
out the lessons of Scripture, but lecturing or reading was largely
concerned with poring over the sacred text. Hence the proud title
accorded Thomas: *magister sacrae paginae* (master of the sacred
page).

God as the subject of supernatural theology

But let us return to Thomas's understanding of *sacra doctrina*, the
theology based on Sacred Scripture. For the reasons given earlier, God
cannot be the subject of a demonstrative or *propter quid* demonstration. In order for this to be the case, we would have to know what
he is, know his definition, but our natural knowledge of God is indirect and oblique, from creatures, and we can only grasp of him what
knowledge of creatures permits us to say. This is an imperfect knowledge, however desirable it may be. In order for his effects to manifest what God is they would have to be commensurate with him,
exhaust his causality, as it were. It would be as if what God has actually created is all he could possibly create and thus provides a window
into his nature. But God is omnipotent. Aristotle said that a little bit

of knowledge, however imperfect, of God is preferable to much perfect knowledge of lesser things. The most striking thing about supernatural theology as Thomas describes it is that in such discourse God is the subject of the science.

Indeed, in contrasting philosophical theology with that based on Scripture, Thomas invokes the Aristotelian distinction between causes that function in the science of the caused which are only treated in that way, and causes which are things in their own right and thus form the subject of a distinct science. (This occurs in his early exposition of Boethius's *On the Trinity*, q. 5, a. 4.) The heavenly bodies thus function as explanatory of terrestrial happenings but are also subjects of a distinct science, astronomy. Philosophical theology is to be found in a science concerned with first causes as explanatory of its subject matter, being as being, metaphysics. Being as being is developed as the subject of a science other than natural science and mathematics to provide a less inadequate access to first causes. Supernatural theology has such first causes as its very subject matter, something possible again only on the basis of truths that have been revealed and which would otherwise be undreamt of by philosophy, e.g., the Trinity, the union of natures in Christ, etc.

For all that, Thomas insists that this does not negate the nature of human understanding, which must always rise to the immaterial from knowledge of the material.

> In our present state of life there is no way we can know the quiddities of immaterial things whether we are speaking of natural knowledge or of revelation, because the light of divine revelation, as Denis says, comes to us according to our own manner of knowing. Hence although revelation elevates us so that we know things we otherwise would not know, we do not know them otherwise than by way of sensible things. (*Exposition of Boethius's On the Trinity*, q. 5, a. 4)

When we consider the images and parables of the Bible the meaning of this reminder is clear. And it leads to a humbling realization.

The paradox of theology

We have had occasion to note the paradoxical fact about Thomas's view of philosophy and its ultimate goal that efforts to know and say things about God exceed our grasp. All such knowledge is oblique and indirect, dependent on sensible things to give us intimations of the divine. Despite the contrast of natural and supernatural theology, this paradox persists.

Following Denis the Areopagite – pseudo-Dionysius – Thomas speaks of three moments or ways in our knowledge of God. There is first the way of similarity, insofar as aspects of creatures tell us something of God. This is also called the way of causality, for obvious reasons. But the affirmations that issue from such arguments – e.g. God is good – are followed by a qualification or *via negationis*: God is not good in the way creatures are: theirs is a derived or participated goodness, he is goodness itself. As to what this means, we can only end by saying that the manner of God's goodness escapes our ability to understand.

We see here the ultimate application of analogy as we have discussed it earlier. Analogous terms are shared terms which have different but related meanings, such that one of the things spoken of is what is primarily meant by the term, and the other understood and named from that primary analogate. This doctrine of analogy permeates Thomas's philosophy from first to last, as we have insisted, and it carries over into the theology based on Sacred Scripture. How are we to understand terms common to God and creature, terms such as being, one, true, good, just, and the like? If as Thomas holds our knowledge begins with the things of sense experience, and if we speak of things insofar as we know them, we first speak of sensible things and that means that such things have first claims on our language. Using our language to speak of sensation, understanding, or love, entails extending terms to them from their native habitat, on the supposition that our knowledge of non-sensible things is dependent on our knowledge of the sensible. This is preeminently true of our talk about God, whether it is engaged in by the philosopher or by the believer in his role as theologian.

All this can be summed up in the phrase that at the end of the theological day we understand that we do not understand God. Why not just call this ignorance rather than negative theology? Why not simply say that we don't know anything about God? The moments and ways just mentioned invite this kind of criticism, and have long received it. Let us develop the criticism before indicating how Thomas would reply to it.

By the way of causality or similitude, we conclude that God is goodness, but then immediately take it away by saying that of course his goodness is not of the same sort as created goodness. Of what sort is it? We don't know. But surely this brings down the whole stack of cards. Perhaps we should just admit that when we speak of God we don't know what we're talking about.

Modesty about our knowledge of God does not preclude a spirited response to this criticism. If we go back to the assumptions of the "way of causality," as exemplified first in any effort to prove the existence of God, the nerve of the effort is located in the demands that knowledge of sensible things makes on us. The proof from motion amounts to the conclusion that the world of moved movers simply could not exist if all movers were moved movers. So there must be an unmoved mover. Now either this inadequacy of the world we know to explain its being there at all is justified or it isn't. If it is, we have a basis for asserting that there is another kind of cause on which the whole shebang depends. The description of God is linked to our knowledge of moved movers – we are denying that he is just another instance of the kind of causes within the world. Nonetheless, we are extrapolating at least the term "cause" to him. A cause is that on which something else depends in order to be. And in the case of God he is not a cause who is himself caused. That is the difference. And again the warrant for saying this is lodged in what we can know of caused causes or moved movers. This dependence on our knowledge of effects never goes away in talking about God. If it is forgotten, talk about God's causality or goodness or justice is simply unanchored. Thomas's denial that we have, whether through natural knowledge or faith, direct insight into the nature of God is always linked with the corresponding claim that knowledge of the things around us forces us to conclude that there must be an unmoved mover, and that is what "God" means. However modest such knowledge, if it is gained in this way, as Thomas thinks it is, philosophically, it does not entail that we know nothing of God, however true it is that we do not have comprehensive knowledge of him, knowledge of his essence. If we did, since his essence is one with his existence, we would of course have no need of any proof.

As for the mysteries of faith, those truths about God which are only accepted as true on the basis of the gift of faith, there are no proofs based on the things that are that can conclude that God is, for example, a trinity of persons. But all of the other restrictions on our knowledge of God are fully in play. In order to make any sense at all of the Trinity, the theologian must clarify what is meant by nature, what is meant by person, what is meant by one, and so forth. These meanings must be found first in creatures and then carefully extended to talk about God. In doing this, the theologian is guided and constrained by what God has told us of himself. "I and the Father are one." That is, his discourse follows from and is dependent upon revelation.

51

The Range of Theology

The only summary of theology Thomas Aquinas completed was his *Summa contra Gentiles*. The *Compendium Theologiae*, which set out to express the nature of Christianity through the three theological virtues, faith, hope, and charity, remained unfinished. And so did his undoubted masterpiece, the *Summa Theologiae*. In his prologue to this work, Thomas expressed dissatisfaction with existing efforts to summarize Christian doctrine, particularly their lack of a planned order which made repetitions necessary. In the *Summa Theologiae* he sought to remedy that defect and to introduce beginners to the subject in a way that would give them a theological *tour du monde*. Although the work remained unfinished at his death, he completed the bulk of it and it is possible to imagine the unwritten portion. Indeed, in the *Supplementum* to the work, editors did just that, cannibalizing Thomas's treatment of the projected topics in his early exposition of the *Sentences* of Peter Lombard.

It may be well to recall the literary form of the *Summa Theologiae*, which is modeled on the disputed questions and differs from both that of the *Summa contra Gentiles* and the *Compendium Theologiae*. The reader of the *Summa*, as we will call it for short, is first struck by its dialectical method. Questions comprise articles and each article obeys a set form in which, a question having been posed and an answer, affirmative or negative, proposed, a series of objections to that answer are set down. Then, in the *sed contra est*, an authority is cited which suggests an answer other than the one posed. There follows the body of the article, in which the alternative answer is discussed and defended, after which the objections to it are addressed. Then on to the next question, and so on through the entire work. The form is meant to convey the way in which the mind works. A question can receive an affirmative or negative answer; there are reasons, however shallow, for accepting one of them, so that the subsequent argument for the opposite answer is developed against an alternative that has commended itself. It is as if a small debate takes place and one side emerges as the victor. But victory opens up the need for further questions, and the activity continues.

In tres partes divisa est

The *Summa* is divided into three unequal parts. The first part contains 119 questions, which can be thought of in terms of 10 treatises. The overall point of the opening part is to begin with God, his nature and attributes, the Trinity, creation and then angels, man and the government of the universe.

The first question of Part One deals with Sacred Doctrine, about which we have said some things earlier (pages 30–1). This is a treatise in itself. The second treatise comprises questions 2 through 26 and is concerned with the one God, the divine nature. In these questions, philosophical proofs of God's existence are recalled and many of the divine attributes discussed have their counterpart in philosophical theology. The suggestion is that such discussions are logically presupposed to the discussion of the mysteries of faith and that recalling them affords a bridge between philosophy and theology.

The third treatise, questions 27 through 43, deals with the trinity of persons in God and the fourth treatise, questions 44–6, discusses the act of creation. This is followed by the fifth, q. 47, dealing with the levels of creation, and the sixth, questions 48–9, which discusses the opposition of good and evil. Questions 50 through 64, the seventh treatise, are devoted to the angels. The eighth treatise, questions 65 through 74, concerns corporeal creation, and the ninth, questions 75 through 102, is the famous Treatise on Man. The tenth treatise, questions 103 through 119, discusses the conservation and governance of the created world.

The First Part of the *Summa* moves off from God into the creation and governance of the world. The Second Part, the largest of the three and divided into halves called the First Part of the Second Part and the Second Part of the Second Part, deals with man's return to God by way of moral and graced action. It remains perhaps the most read and discussed part of this massive work. In the prologue, Thomas explains that man is said to be created in the image of God because he has a reason and will and thus alone of bodily creatures is able to take a free and responsible part in achieving his own destiny. The First Part of the Second comprises eight treatises which deal with moral matters at a high level of generality. The first treatise is made up of questions 1 through 5, which discuss man's ultimate end and happiness, union with God. We have already seen how these questions subsume the philosophical discussion of these matters and complete them by stressing man's supernatural end. The second treatise, questions 6 through 21, provides a discussion of human acts, the subject matter of moral theology. Questions 22 through 48, the third treatise, discuss the emotions or passions which are the matter of the moral virtues. Sensation is the source of appetitive moves of attraction and repulsion which are not yet moral; only as directed by reason and thus become responsible do they have moral valence. The fourth treatise, questions 49 through 54, discusses the nature and acquisition of habits, and the fifth treatise, questions 55 through 70, discusses the virtues. Questions 71 through 89, the sixth treatise, are concerned with vice and sin. The Treatise on Law, the much discussed seventh treatise, runs from question 90 through 108 and contains Thomas's discussion of natural law as well as of the decalogue. The eighth and final treatise of this subpart, questions 109 through 114, deals with grace.

The Second Part of the Second Part contains a more detailed discussion of the virtues and their various subdivisions, and comprises ten treatises. The first, questions 1 through 16, deals with the first of the theological virtues, faith; the second, questions 17 through 22, considers hope; and the third, questions 23 through 46, charity. These are followed by discussions of the cardinal virtues. The fourth treatise, questions 47 through 56, deals with prudence or practical wisdom; the fifth, questions 57 through 122, with justice; the sixth, questions, 123 through 140, with fortitude or courage; the seventh, questions 141 through 170, with temperance. These discussions ingeniously include discussions of the beatitudes and the gifts of the Holy Ghost. The eighth treatise, questions 171 through 178, considers graces gratuitously given, and the ninth, questions 179 through 182, deals with the active and contemplative lives. Finally, the tenth treatise, questions 183 through 189, considers the various offices and conditions of men.

The Third Part of the *Summa* concerns Christ and the means instituted for our salvation. Of it we have six treatises, the last unfinished. The first treatise, questions 1 through 59, deals with the Incarnation. The second, questions 60 through 65, with sacraments in general, after which discussions of the particular sacraments follow. The third treatise, questions 68 through 71, deals with baptism; the fourth, question 72, with confirmation; the fifth, questions 73 through 83, with the Eucharist. The sixth, of which we have questions 84 through 90, deals with the sacrament of penance. As has been mentioned, the plan of the *Summa* was completed by later editors from earlier writings of Thomas. Questions 1 through 28 of the *Supplementum* give what is wanting in the treatise on penance. Questions 29 through 33 discuss extreme unction, the anointing of the sick, the last rites, and questions 34 through 40 discuss Holy Orders. Matrimony is discussed in questions 41 and 68, and questions 69 through 99 deal with the resurrection and the four last things.

It is customary to remark on and praise the ordering of this vast amount of doctrine and comparisons have been made to the proportions and beauty of the medieval cathedral. The *Summa* was enshrined on the altar with the Bible at the sessions of the Council of Trent. Reading it becomes addictive, not least because of its dialectical method which introduces the reader to an ongoing conversation, and one is reluctant to withdraw. Because of the way in which theology, as Thomas understands it, employs and subsumes philosophical discussions, the *Summa* is often mined for its philosophical discussions without reference to the theological purpose to which they are put. Indeed, since Thomas often worked up the philosophical presuppositions in a succinct way here, as he never does elsewhere, the *Summa* is rightly seen as a source book for his philosophy as well as his theology. But in itself it is a monument to the Christian wisdom which builds on philosophy and soars far beyond it.

SOURCES

Chapter 11   Theology Presupposes Philosophy

Summa Theologiae, I, question 1, article 1 (translated by Thomas Gilby OP. Oxford: Blackfriars, 1963). The prologue to Thomas's exposition of the *Sentences* of Peter Lombard is an earlier treatment of many of the same questions.

Chapter 12   The Quest of Philosophy

Thomas's commentary on the opening chapters of Book One of the *Metaphysics* (translated and introduced by John P. Rowan, preface by Ralph McInerny. South Bend: Dumb Ox Books, 1995).

Chapter 13   Theoretical and Practical

Commentary on Aristotle's De Anima, Book 3, lesson 15 (translated by Kenelm Foster OP and Silvester Humphries OP, introduction by Ralph McInerny. South Bend: Dumb Ox Books, 1994). For degrees of practical thought, see *Summa Theologiae*, I, question 14, article 16.

Chapter 14   The Order of Learning

Commentary on the Book of Causes, preface (translated by Vincent Guagliardo OP, Charles Hess OP, and Richard Taylor. Washington: Catholic University of America Press, 1996). Also in Penguin Classic *Thomas Aquinas: Selected Writings*, edited and translated with an introduction and notes by Ralph McInerny. London: Penguin Books, 1998.

Chapter 15   The Two Theologies

Other than the texts cited, see Thomas's exposition on Boethius's *On the Trinity*, question 5, article 4 and question 6, article 4, *Faith, Reason and Theology* (translation by Armand Mauer, CSB. Toronto: PIMS, 1987).

Chapter 16   The Four Orders

Commentary on Aristotle's Nicomachean Ethics (translated by C. I. Litzinger OP, foreword by Ralph McInerny. South Bend: Dumb Ox

Books, 1993). See also the prooemia to Thomas's comentaries on the *De Interpretatione* and *Posterior Analytics* (Jean Oesterle, Milwaukee: Marquette University Press, 1975).

Chapter 17   The Logical Order

For the distinction of *ens rationis* and *ens naturae*, see *Aquinas On Being and Essence: A Translation and Interpretation*, by Joseph Bobik. Notre Dame: University of Notre Dame Press, 1965. See too the *Commentary on the Metaphysics*, Book Five, lesson 9.

Chapter 18   Our Natural Way of Knowing

See Thomas's *Commentary on Aristotle's Physics* (translated by Richard Blackwell, Richard Spath, and W. Edmund Thirkel, introduction by Vernon Bourke, foreword by Ralph McInerny. South Bend: Dumb Ox Books, 1999). See also *Summa Theologiae*, I, question 85.

Chapter 19   Matter and Form

Commentary on Aristotle's Physics, Book One, lessons 11 and 12. *On the Principles of Nature* (in Penguin Classics, *Thomas Aquinas: Selected Writings*, and also in Joseph Bobik, *Aquinas on Matter and Form*, Notre Dame: University of Notre Dame Press, 1998.)

Chapter 20   Things that Come to Be as the Result of a Change

Commentary on Aristotle's Physics, Book One, lesson 11 through 13.

Chapter 21   The Parmenidean Problem

Commentary on Aristotle's Physics, Book One, lesson 14.

Chapter 22   The Sequel

Commentary on Aristotle's On Sense and the Sensed Object, prologue.

Chapter 23   The Prime Mover

Commentary on Aristotle's Physics, Book Eight (South Bend: Dumb Ox Books, 1999). See the summary of the proof in *Summa contra*

Gentiles, Book One, chapters 9–14 (in *Thomas Aquinas: Selected Writings*, translated and edited, with an introduction and notes, by Ralph McInerny. London: Penguin Books, 1998), and in *Summa Theologiae*, question 2, article 3.

Chapter 24   The Soul

Commentary on Aristotle's De Anima, Book Two, lessons 1 through 5. (in *Thomas Aquinas: Selected Writings*, translated and edited, with an introduction and notes, by Ralph McInerny. London: Penguin Books, 1998).

Chapter 25   Sense Perception

Commentary on Aristotle's De Anima, Book Two, lessons 10 through 13. *Summa Theologiae*, I, question 78, articles 3 and 4.

Chapter 26   The Immortality of the Human Soul

Commentary on Aristotle's De Anima, Book Three, lessons 4, 7 through 9. *Summa Theologiae*, I, question 76. *Aquinas against the Averroists: On There Being Only One Intellect* (translated with introduction and notes by Ralph McInerny. Lafayette: Purdue University Press, 1993).

Chapter 27   The Opening to Metaphysics

Exposition of Boethius's On the Trinity, question 5, articles 3 and 4.

Chapter 28   The Big Problem

See John Wippel, *The Metaphysical Thought of Thomas Aquinas*, Washington: Catholic University of America Press, 2000, Part One, chapters iii and iv.

Chapter 29   The Two Theologies Revisited

See Armand Mauer, *Faith, Reason and Theology*, Toronto, PIMS, 1987.

Chapter 30   Being as Being

Commentary on Aristotle's Metaphysics, Book Four, lesson 1. *Exposition of Boethius's On the Trinity*, question 5, article 4, question 6, article 4. *Aquinas On Being and Essence*.

Chapter 31   Analogy

Summa Theologiae, I, question 13, articles 5 and 6. Ralph McInerny, *Aquinas and Analogy* (Washington: Catholic University of America Press, 1996).

Chapter 32   Being as Analogous

Commentary on Aristotle's Metaphysics, Book Four, lessons 1 and 2.

Chapter 33   Substance

Commentary on Aristotle's Metaphysics, Book Five, lesson 9, Book Seven, lessons 1 and 2.

Chapter 34   Presuppositions of Metaphysics

Exposition of Boethius's On the Trinity, question 5, articles 1 through 4.

Chapter 35   God and Metaphysics

Exposition of Boethius's On the Trinity, question 5, article 4, question 6, article 4. *Commentary on the Metaphysics of Aristotle*, Book Twelve, lesson 5 through 8.

Chapter 36   Ipsum esse Subsistens

Exposition of Boethius's De Hebdomadibus, lesson 2. *Summa Theologiae*, question 13, article 11.

Chapter 37   The Moral Order

Commentary on Aristotle's Nicomachean Ethics, Book One, lesson 1. *Summa Theologiae*, First Part of the Second Part, question 1.

Chapter 38   Ultimate End in Aristotle

Commentary on Aristotle's Nicomachean Ethics, Book One, lesson 2.

Chapter 39   Ultimate End in Thomas

Summa Theologiae, First Part of the Second Part, question 1.

Chapter 40   Virtuous Action

Disputed Questions on Virtue (translation and preface by Ralph McInerny. South Bend: St Augustine's Press, 1998). *Summa Theologiae*, First Part of the Second Part, questions 55 through 60.

Chapter 41   Natural Law

Summa Theologiae, First Part of the Second Part, questions 90 and 94 (in Penguin Classics, *Aquinas*).

Chapter 42   Natural Inclinations

Summa Theologiae, First Part of the Second Part, question 94, article 2.

Chapter 43   Virtue and Law

Ralph McInerny, *Ethica Thomistica* (revised edn. Washington: Catholic University of America Press, 1997).

Chapter 44   Practical Syllogism

Commentary on Aristotle's Nicomachean Ethics, Book Seven, lessons 2 and 3. *Summa Theologiae*, First Part of Second Part, question 13, article 1.

Chapter 45   End/Means

Summa Theologiae, First Part of Second Part, questions 13 through 16.

Chapter 46   The Common Good

Commentary on Aristotle's Nicomachean Ethics, Book Six, lesson 7. *Commentary on Aristotle's Metaphysics*, Book Twelve, lesson 12. *Summa Theologiae*, First Part, question 44, article 4.

Chapter 47   Natural and Supernatural Ends

Summa Theologiae, First Part of Second Part, question 3; First Part, question 12.

Chapter 48   Preambles of Faith

Exposition of Boethius's On the Trinity, questions 1 and 2 (in Penguin Classics, *Aquinas*).

Chapter 49   Christian Philosophy

Leo XIII, *Aeterni Patris*; John Paul II, *Fides et Ratio*; Ralph McInerny, *Characters in Search of Their Author* (Notre Dame: University of Notre Dame Press, 2001).

Chapter 50   Beyond Philosophy

Summa Theologiae, I, question one, article one. *Exposition of Boethius's On the Trinity*, question six, article four.

Chapter 51   The Range of Theology

John of St Thomas, *Introduction to the Summa Theologiae of Thomas Aquinas* (translation and introduction by Ralph McInerny. South Bend: St Augustine's Press, 2003).

SELECTED FURTHER READING

Bobik, Joseph. *Veritas Divina: Aquinas on Divine Truth*. South Bend: St Augustine's Press, 2001.

Burrell, David. *Freedom and Creation in Three Traditions*. Notre Dame: University of Notre Dame Press, 1993.

Copleston, F. C. *Aquinas*. London: Penguin Books, 1955.

Elders, Leo. *The Philosophy of Nature of St. Thomas Aquinas*. Frankfurt: Peter Lang, 1997.

Fabro, Cornelio. *Le prove dell'esistenza di Dio*. Brescia: La Scuola, 1989.

Flannery, Kevin. *Acts amid Precepts: The Aristotelian Logical Structure of Aquinas's Moral Theory*. Washington: Catholic University of America Press, 2001.

Hibbs, Thomas S. *Dialectic and Narrative in Aquinas: An Interpretation of the Summa contra Gentiles*. Notre Dame: University of Notre Dame Press, 1995.

Jenkins John J. *Knowledge and Faith in Thomas Aquinas*. Cambridge: Cambridge University Press, 1997.

Maritain, Jacques. *The Degrees of Knowledge*. Notre Dame: University of Notre Dame Press, 1995.

McInerny, Ralph. *Thomas Aquinas: Selected Writings*. London: Penguin Classics, 1998.

McInerny, Ralph. *Boethius and Aquinas*. Washington: Catholic University of America Press, 1990.

McInerny, Ralph. *Aquinas and Analogy*. Washington: Catholic University of America Press, 1996.

O'Callaghan, John and Hibbs, Thomas. *Recovering Nature*. Notre Dame: University of Notre Dame Press, 1999.

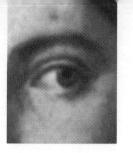

— Part III —

Thomism

While a thinker would have to be obscure indeed not to qualify as the object of historical research or a doctoral dissertation, there are few figures in the history of philosophy who remain as active participants in ongoing philosophical inquiries. There are Plato scholars, but there are Platonists as well, contemporaries of ours; there are Aristotle scholars, but there are Aristotelians, thinkers who 2,500 years after the death of the Stagirite learn from and debate with him as if he were in the room. There are a few other such figures as well, perhaps half a dozen in all. Thomas Aquinas is one of them. There are Thomists among us even now.

People have debated what the term "Thomist" means. How can you identify a philosopher as a Thomist? A preliminary distinction is that already mentioned, between historical research into a thinker and regarding a thinker as a participant in the ongoing philosophical quest. There are many medievalists who do research on Thomas Aquinas, and the results of their inquiry are of enormous value to those interested in Thomas in the second sense. Etienne Gilson once made the following comparison between himself and Jacques Maritain.

> The last book of Maritain is of decisive importance for a correct under-standing of his thought. Its reading made me realize that *I had never understood his true position.* I was naively maintaining that one cannot consider oneself a Thomist without first ascertaining the authentic meaning of St. Thomas's doctrine, which only history can do; during all that time, he was considering himself a true disciple of St. Thomas because he was *continuing* his thought.*

Etienne Gilson and Jacques Maritain were without any doubt two of the major figures in the revival of Thomism initiated by Leo XIII's 1879 encyclical *Aeterni Patris*. Their names were so often linked that they might have seemed like two ends of the same thought, but as in the case of Chesterton and Belloc, the two men did not see a great deal of one another, and their mutual admiration was sustained by a saving distance. In the letter quoted Gilson is writing at the age of 89 and he could be said to have

---

* Gilson, letter to Father Armand Maurer included in *Etienne Gilson/Jacques Maritain Correspondance 1923–1971* (ed. Géry Prouvost. Paris: J. Vrin, 1991, p. 275).

become a victim of so-called Irish Alzheimer's – one forgets every-thing except the grudges. Gilson's late letters are replete with pot shots but this comparison of himself and Maritain is of enormous importance for understanding the role that Thomas Aquinas played in twentieth-century philosophy, both European and American. But before turning to that, we must at least sketch the history of Thomism prior to 1879.

It is customary to divide that history into two major periods, the first from the thirteenth through the sixteenth century, the second from the sixteenth to the modern Thomistic revival. Other more fine-grained divisions have been proposed.**

**   For a discussion of the various divisions, see Romanus Cessario, *Le Thomisme et les Thomistes* (Paris: Cerf, 1999).

52

The First Phase

We saw in Part I that in the controversy over Latin Averroism some saw Thomas's attitude toward Aristotle as equally suspicious, despite his own definitive refutation of the heterodox Aristotelianism of some masters in the faculty of arts at Paris. In 1270, Etienne Tempier, bishop of Paris, condemned positions associated with Latin Averroism, none of which implicated Thomas. But in 1277, at the behest of Peter of Spain, now Pope John XXI, Tempier condemned 219 propositions among which are to be found undoubted teachings of Thomas Aquinas who had died three years earlier. This brought the septuagenarian Albert the Great to Paris to defend his former student and declare that Thomas "had been the flower and adornment of the world: *fuerat flos et decus mundi.*" Indeed, this condemnation had the effect of consolidating the Order of Preachers who were to make the teaching of the doctrine of Thomas mandatory in the studia of the Order. Whether or not it be attributed to the eventual anti-Aristotelianism of Bonaventure, Franciscans went on the attack against Thomas.

In England there was division among the Dominicans themselves. Robert Kilwardby, Dominican and archbishop of Canterbury, considered some of Thomas's teachings heretical, but it would be English Dominicans who came to Thomas's defense when the Franciscans went on the attack. John Peckham is thought to have been the target of Thomas's little work *On the Eternity of the World*. This Franciscan would become archbishop of Canterbury as successor to Kilwardby, and he made clear that the Parisian condemnation applied to Oxford and Cambridge. The next phase of the battle was English. The Franciscan William de la Mare, perhaps at Peckham's suggestion, produced shortly after the condemnation a work entitled *Correctorium Fratris Thomae: Critique of Brother Thomas* aimed at refuting tenets of Thomism that went counter to the teachings of Bonaventure and Augustine. The reading of the *Summa Theologiae* was sharply curtailed in Franciscan houses. Dominican responses swiftly followed with *Correctoria Corruptorii: Critiques of the Distortions*, two by the Englishmen Richard Knapwell and Thomas Sutton, a third by a French Dominican with the somnolent sobriquet of Jean Quidort.

The Paris condemnation was officially revoked on February 14, 1325, two years after Thomas's canonization. However, these posthumous attacks on Thomas had the effect of establishing him as a hero for Dominicans. Kilwardby and later Durandus almost exhaust the list of anti-Thomist Dominicans. For Franciscans, on the other hand, opposition to Thomas's teaching was *de rigueur*. Philosophical schools are always mixed blessings but when allegiance to a religious order is added to the mix, and the enemy identified, endless controversy is guaranteed. Of course, this is not to say that the disputes were over insignificant matters or to deny that one side had the better of the argument. But an accompanying intransigence all but rules out attending to the opponent on the chance that he might be right and one might therefore have to change one's mind. Worse, philosophy and theology came to seem less the common effort to arrive at the truth than moving within the assumptions of a school or sect. Now there would be Thomists and Scotists and Ockhamists, the differences proliferating and becoming ever more arcane, anticipating the fracturing of Christianity in the Reformation and the multiplication of philosophies in the modern era.

The opponents of Thomas regarded him as a foe of the tradition they claimed to defend, which had its roots in the thought of St Augustine. The influence of Aristotle on Thomas's thinking was taken to lead to positions inimical to the Augustinian tradition. (It should be said that some historians regard this "tradition" as invented ad hoc as a weapon against the new learning.) No reader of Thomas would find anything but the greatest deference to Augustine, though of course Thomas's was a critical reception. But then, in retrospect, Augustine in the *Retractationes* was critical of himself. The point was not loyalty to Augustine, but to the truth. *Magis amicus veritas.*

The situation was complicated by the theological implications of philosophical positions. Thomas taught that a substance has but one substantial form and in the human being it is the soul. This was objected to, not on the philosophical grounds given, but because it was supposed that, if true, it would prevent our talking of Christ's body in the tomb before Easter morning. Was it not something? Did that not require a form? Must there not be, then, a plurality of substantial forms?

To bring a philosophical tenet to the bar of the faith has often spurred philosophical thought to realizations that might otherwise have been overlooked. This is the great contention of Etienne Gilson's *The Spirit of Mediaeval Philosophy*. But the often precipitous conclusion that a philosophical position runs afoul of the faith and is heretical, when made by one thinker to another, believers both, can be a species of bullying. Official condemnations are another thing, but even they can reflect the opacity of the private intimidator, as witness the condemnation of some Thomistic tenets in 1277.

The unhappy result was that the philosophy of Thomas, which he did not regard as a *kind* of philosophy – a sign of which is his treatment of Neoplatonic texts – came to be regarded as such, even by its defenders. Meanwhile, Scotus and Ockham, whose mission was to overthrow Thomism in both philosophy and theology, led the way toward nominalism and fideism.

In the fourteenth century Herveus Natalis countered the anti-Thomism of the Dominican Durandus, and in the fifteenth century John Capreolus (1444), *princeps thomistarum* (the chief of Thomists), defended the theology of Thomas against Scotist attacks, while Peter of Bergamo in the sixteenth century wrote a *Tabula Aurea*, a Thomistic index that continues to be of great use to students of St Thomas. Sylvester of Ferrara wrote a commentary on the *Summa contra Gentiles* which accompanies the Leonine edition of that work. And Thomas de Vio Cardinal Cajetan, who had been sent by the pope to meet with Martin Luther, wrote a commentary on the *Summa Theologiae* which is included in the Leonine edition of Thomas's *chef d'oeuvre*. Cajetan taught in Italy, became master general of the Dominicans, and in retreat at Gaeta wrote a series of biblical commentaries influenced by the new trends in scriptural interpretation.

53

Second Scholasticism

The center of gravity of Thomism shifted to Spain although the Iberian flourishing of Thomism, often called the Second Scholasticism, had received its impetus in Paris where the Belgian Peter Crockhaert taught Francisco de Vitoria, one of the stars of the invigorated Thomism that centered in the University of Salamanca. Melchior Cano played a key role at the Council of Trent, called to confront the challenge of the Reformation. John of St Thomas (Jean Poinsot) gave a new impetus to the study of Thomas which had been eclipsed in the older universities because of the influence of nominalism. In his *Cursus Philosophicus* John gave a summary of philosophy in which he defended positions taught by Thomas against latter-day criticisms. His massive *Cursus Theologicus* follows the order of the *Summa Theologiae* and is also characterized by a continuing debate between rival positions. Dominic Banez, another Dominican, spiritual advisor of Teresa of Avila, commented on the *Summa*, and at Salamanca Francesco de Vitoria and other Dominicans carried on the Thomistic tradition with vigor, addressing, *inter alia*, problems raised by the Spanish colonization of the New World. Vitoria is known as the father of international law. Also at Salamanca, the Jesuit Francisco Suarez, a thinker of enormous power and Thomist of a sort, wrote his *Metaphysical Disputations* which can be said to assimilate everything that had gone before and shape it into a form it had not had. His is said to be the first independent metaphysical treatise, as opposed to commentary on Aristotle's *Metaphysics*. It is largely through Suarez that late scholasticism influenced the new mode of philosophizing that began with Descartes. The Jesuits and Dominicans entered into lively debate on questions related to divine foreknowledge and the free acts of human agents, as earlier Franciscans and Dominicans had disagreed on the Immaculate Conception of the Blessed Virgin Mary.

The history of Thomism takes place against the background of political upheavals and Church history, the Avignon papacy, the Reformation, the Council of Trent, the defeat of the Spanish Armada, the French Revolution, and the Napoleonic era. Throughout these developments, Thomas played a role. Along with the Bible, the *Summa Theologiae* was placed on the altar around which the discussions of Trent took place. The niceties of this continuation of the role of Thomas must be left to historians. Our emphasis must be on the revival initiated by Leo XIII.

54

The Leonine Revival (1879–1965)

When John Henry Newman came to Rome shortly after his conversion to Catholicism, he found little in the way of Thomism. No one would openly attack the teaching of Thomas, he was told, but practically it was a dead letter. How true this was is perhaps less important than the impression created. It was as if you could shoot a cannon through Rome and never hit a Thomist. But the seeds of what was about to happen were being planted in various places, notably Naples (Gaetano Sanseverino), and they involved Jesuits (the brothers Sordi, Serafino and Domenico) as well as Dominicans. At the Jesuit university in Rome, Matteo Liberatore and Josef Kleutgen spurred the new emphasis. Prior to his election as pope, Leo and his brother Giuseppe Pecci were involved in a revival of the study of Thomas in Perugia, Leo's then see. The clear affirmation of the relationship between faith and reason provided by Vatican I played its role. When he was elected pope, Leo founded the Pontifical Roman Academy of St Thomas, with his brother as head, and in 1879 issued the encyclical, called from its opening Latin words *Aeterni Patris*. It soon came to be known as the document that called for the restoration of the study of Thomas Aquinas in the Catholic schools.

Leo's intention cannot be understood without taking into account the parlous condition of the Church in an increasingly secularized Europe. In Germany, the *Kulturkampf* under Bismarck persecuted the Church, and other political currents would soon seek to marginalize

Catholicism in such countries as France, called the eldest daughter of the Church. Religious orders would be driven into exile as the secularization of the schools was completed. Leo XIII's opposition to political liberalism, like that of Newman in a famous appendix to his *Apologia pro Vita Sua*, went hand in hand with alarm at the inroads of liberalism into the understanding of the Christian faith. Leo saw the origins of political and theological errors in the course philosophy had taken in the modern world, and his encyclical was meant to provide the intellectual counter to that development. What was needed was a robust renewal of the Christian wisdom that had been developed over the centuries from the earliest days of the Church, but was now eclipsed by the events alluded to.

It should be noted that, although Leo's encyclical brought about the revival of Thomas among Catholics, Thomas was not so much as mentioned until well into the document. Indeed, Thomas was presented as the paladin of a Christian philosophy to which all the great figures of Church history had contributed. The mark of Thomas was that he was, as it were, a personal *summa* of all that had gone before, and thus a model of what must be done in order to provide an intellectual alternative to those tenets of modernity which were at odds with Christian faith.

The response to *Aeterni Patris* was eventually global, giving new impetus to the study of the philosophy and theology of Thomas Aquinas. New schools were founded, as well as new journals and societies. Curricula were developed which implemented the aims of the encyclical. Non-Catholics unaware of the points made earlier in Part Two were undoubtedly puzzled by all this. Thomas was put forward under the aegis of the Church and with frequent approbation by the papal magisterium. Thomas Aquinas was clearly regarded as the Catholic intellectual champion, but how could philosophy be promoted in the context of religious faith? Eventually, great attention would be given to the concept of Christian philosophy, with results that were often ambiguous.

Independently of all this, but increasingly affected by it, was the revival of scholarly interest in the Middle Ages. In France, quite secular scholars became interested in medieval philosophy and they were to be joined and then surpassed by the enormous contributions of Etienne Gilson, whose course in the thought of Thomas would become his work, *Le Thomisme*, which would develop through many editions to trace the evolving understanding of Thomas by Gilson himself. Gilson exerted equal if not perhaps greater influence in North

America, where he founded the Pontifical Institute of Mediaeval Studies, and divided his academic year between Toronto and Paris. Jacques Maritain also taught in Toronto, but was never the permanent member of the Institute that Gilson wished him to be. Like Gilson, he alternated between Paris and America. Other centers of Thomism in North America were at Laval University in Quebec, where the dean of the faculté de philosophie, Charles DeKoninck, influenced a generation of Thomists, and Ottawa, where the Dominicans flourished. In the United States, the Catholic University of America, St Louis University, and the University of Notre Dame, developed graduate programs which would provide teachers for the Catholic colleges of the nation.

The undoubtedly Catholic character of these developments puzzled those who had come to think of philosophy as completely secular, not subject to the influence of religious faith and, indeed, inimical to it. How could a Christian believer follow the argument wherever it went as, by supposition, the secular thinker did? All this came to a head in the controversy over Christian philosophy that was precipitated in the early 1930s by an article of the historian of philosophy, Emile Brehier, which asked if there was any such thing as Christian philosophy. His answer was no. Philosophizing that was guided and influenced by Christian faith was simply not philosophy. Theology, yes; philosophy, no. The French Thomist Society, meeting at Juvisy, addressed this charge and brought together most of the famous or soon-to-be famous French Catholic philosophers.

Shortly before this meeting, Gilson had delivered his magnificent Gifford lectures, which were published as *The Spirit of Mediaeval Philosophy*. Gilson argued that it was undeniable that certain philosophical advances had been made under the impetus of Christian faith which arguably would not otherwise have been made. A favorite example was the concept of person, which had been clarified in efforts to understand the Incarnation and Trinity. The suggestion was that, although this was the setting in which such philosophical advances had been made, they were tenable on their own merits and without reference to the theological impetus. On this understanding, the relationship between the philosophical innovation and religious faith was contingent and historical and not essential.

A case can be made that the revival of Thomism set in motion by Leo XIII effectively came to an end with Vatican II (1962–5). This was not because of anything said in the conciliar documents – Thomas continued to be pointed to as mentor and guide and the chain of papal recommendations of him continued unbroken – but, as with so many things in the post-conciliar period, the "Spirit of Vatican II" was invoked and said to have ended the hegemony of Thomism. What is undeniable is that Thomists went over the walls, so to speak, with something of the same rapidity and numbers as priests and nuns were to desert their vocations. In the third millennium, a new phase of the history of Thomism seems to be under way. But before turning to that, a word about the pre-conciliar situation.

The influence of Thomas Aquinas has been long and continuous, at least in the Dominican Order. The Church has repeatedly recommended him as mentor in philosophy and theology, as the documents collected by John of St Thomas in the seventeenth century attest. For all that, it can be said that it was only with the issuance of Leo XIII's *Aeterni Patris* at the end of the nineteenth century that Thomas became a dominant figure, first among Catholics and then, as the Thomistic revival progressed, generally among friend and foe alike.

55

Three Thomisms

There have been many efforts to characterize the shapes and forms of Thomism as the Leonine revival crested.* I propose a threefold division: transcendental Thomism, existential Thomism, and Aristotelian Thomism.

Transcendental Thomism may be roughly characterized as based on the belief that the Kantian critique is justified. Consequently, if Thomism is to gain a hearing from a world in which that view of Kant is shared, a post-critical Thomas must be fashioned. Marcechal can be considered the father of this movement, which includes such figures as Karl Rahner and Bernard Lonergan, all Jesuits. Maurice

---

* Mention has been made of Romano Cessario's *Le Thomisme et les Thomistes*. There is also Géry Prouvost's *Thomas d'Aquin et les Thomismes* (Paris: Cerf, 1996), which I will not characterize as tendentious since my own sketch is doubtless open to the same charge.

Blondel's influence on Henri de Lubac is a variant of transcendental Thomism. To simplify even further, transcendental Thomism, having abandoned epistemological realism, seeks to find in the workings of the human mind warrant for objective truths. This type of Thomism is favored by theologians rather than philosophers, as even its proponents acknowledge.

Existential Thomism, while it bears some incidental relation to postwar Existentialism, is based upon the conviction that the real composition of essence and existence in everything but God is the *clef de voute* of Thomism. Etienne Gilson and Cornelio Fabro are the giants of this school, but there are significant differences between them. What is shared is the assumption that the distinction of essence and existence provides a warrant for metaphysics without any dependence on a philosophy of nature. Peculiar to Gilson is his insistence that the order of theology is the order of philosophy for Thomas and that his relation to Aristotle is ultimately antagonistic. In the eyes of critics, existential Thomism, in its final Gilsonian phases, is the abandonment of philosophy in favor of a Christian philosophy indistinguishable from theology.

Aristotelian Thomism is exemplified in Part II of this presentation. It seems to me clearly to be the most faithful and fruitful approach to Thomas. Moreover, by emphasizing the autonomy of philosophy – though of course for the believer philosophizing is never separate from his faith – it is better able to enter the wider philosophical marketplace. Of course, Aristotle is not in the ascendancy in contemporary philosophy, though he remains a permanent point of reference. Obviously, there are merits in the other approaches to Thomas, and it is a mark of Aristotelian Thomism that it is always on the *qui vive* for such merits since it aspires to assimilate in the principled way of Thomas himself.

It may be noted that theologians often complain that there has been a tendency to make Thomas into a pure philosopher and ignore the fact that he was by profession a theologian. The counter concern is also heard, that stressing Thomas as theologian has the unfortunate effect of estranging him from ongoing philosophizing. The answer to both these concerns is to be found in Thomas himself, as the discussion of the relationship between philosophy and theology in Part II (chapters 29, 47–51) should show.

56

Whither Thomism in the Third Millennium?

If we have learned anything in the past few decades it is that our ability to foresee what lies around the corner of time is severely limited. Who would have thought in the heyday of Thomism, at the midpoint of the twentieth century, that the wholesale abandonment of Thomas's doctrine by individuals and institutions lay just ahead? That abandonment, if that is not too strong a term, has had the effect of releasing Thomas into the wider scholarly and philosophical scene, into the public domain. No longer is a person's interest in Thomas taken as prima facie evidence that he is on the verge of conversion to Catholicism – always of course a consummation devoutly to be wished. Unprompted by ecclesiastic approval, any number of philosophers have been drawn to the texts of Thomas. Medieval studies has continued its amazing advance into the third millennium, but not all interest in Thomas is of a historical nature. To invoke Gilson's distinction in the letter cited at the outset of this part (p. 139), Maritain-like as well as Gilsonian interest in Thomas is to be found in the most surprising places. We seem to have entered a phase of its history that could be called freelance Thomism.

Once there were graduate programs fashioned to lead the neophyte into the arcana of Thomas's thought, programs that were, *ut ita dicam*, both Gilsonian and Maritain-like in their aims. Nowadays, many graduate programs in philosophy feature a Thomist, even two, sometimes as exotic novelties, often on the zoological principle followed by Noah in filling the ark. But even if there be but one, breeding occurs and a new generation of freelance Thomists is generated. Their sires – or dames – are sometimes remnants of the Leonine Israel long since dispersed. But as often as not these professors are autodidacts rather than disciples of a master or mistress. Once Thomists had organizations and journals and meetings in which to disagree with one another. Now there is something like a secret handshake by which the scattered devotees acknowledge one another.

What is lacking in this diaspora is any sense of representing a minority view, an odd speciality tolerated by the dominant secular trends in philosophy. It remains a mark of the Thomist that he does not consider himself to be engaged in a *kind* of philosophy. A remarkable statement of that conviction can be found in John Paul II's *Fides et Ratio*, the *Aeterni Patris* of our times. The pope begins, as presentations of Philosophy 101 often do, with the observation that philosophical questions, far from being the puzzles of the sophisticated few, represent large issues no one can fail to face sooner or later. In that sense, everyone is a philosopher by dint of being a human being. But then the question of the variety and rivalry of philosophical systems is raised, and the encyclical suggests something extremely important. It is not simply that there are certain questions no human person can fail to ask. There are shared answers to those questions.

> Although times change and knowledge increases, it is possible to discern a core of philosophical insight within the history of thought as a whole. Consider, for example, the principles of non-contradiction, finality and causality, as well as the concept of the person as a free and intelligent subject, with the capacity to know God, truth and goodness. Consider as well certain fundamental moral norms which are shared by all. These are among the indications that, beyond different schools of thought, there exists a body of knowledge which may be judged a kind of spiritual heritage of humanity. It is as if we had come upon an *implicit philosophy*, as a result of which all feel they possess these principles, albeit in a general and unreflective way. (para. 4)

In Part II (chapter 18) we spoke of the pre-philosophical starting points or principles that Thomas assumes as already known and as non-gainsayable. Surely this is what is being referred to in the passage just quoted. It continues: "Precisely because it is shared in some measure by all, this knowledge should serve as a kind of reference point for the different philosophical schools." This is a succinct statement of the attitude that seems to characterize Thomists now as before. If I have been successful in presenting Thomas's world view in Part II, the reader will understand why the more or less technical vocabulary that is developed is anything but a jargon, some patois that separates the speaker from the mass of mankind. All philosophers long to be intelligible, perhaps, but the recognition that such intelligibility requires a warm and continuous relation to the

knowledge every human person at least implicitly has is not universally recognized. It is the boast of the Thomist, alas often undercut
by his practice, that what he puts forward in argument is the efflo-
rescence of what *Fides et Ratio* calls "implicit philosophy."

SELECTED FURTHER READING

Cessario, Romanus. *Le Thomisme et les Thomistes*. Paris: Cerf, 1999.

Fabro, Cornelio. *Introduzione a San Tommaso*. Milan: Edizioni Ares, 1983.

Gilson, Etienne. *The Philosopher and Theology*. New York: Random House, 1962.

Knasas, John, *Being and Some Twentieth Century Thomists*, New York: Fordham University Press, 2003.

McCool, Gerald. *The Neo-Thomists*. Milwaukee: Marquette University Press, 1994.

McInerny, Ralph. *Thomism in an Age of Renewal*. New York: Doubleday, 1965.

Nichols, Aidan. *Catholic Thought since the Enlightenment*. Pretoria: University of South Africa, 1998.

Prouvost, Géry. *Thomas d'Aquin et les Thomismes*. Paris: Cerf, 1996.

Index